NOTTING HILL GATE 1

Klassenarbeitstrainer

Erarbeitet von

Eva Cloer (Bremen),
Katrin Kremer (Hückeswagen),
Katja Werthen-Giles (Oyten)

Diesterweg

NOTTING HILL GATE 1

Für Klasse 5 an Gesamtschulen und anderen integrierenden Schulformen

Materialien für Schülerinnen und Schüler

- Textbook 978-3-425-14001-8
- Workbook mit Lernsoftware und Audio-CD 978-3-425-14021-6
- Workbook mit Audio-CD 978-3-425-14011-7
- Lernsoftware mit Einzelplatzlizenz 978-3-425-14051-3
- Vocab-App (Android-Version) WEB-425-14061
- Vocab-App (iOS-Version) WEB-425-13965
- Trainingsheft Besser lesen 978-3-425-14031-5
- Inklusions- und Fördermaterialien mit Audio-CD 978-3-425-14671-3
- Zoom-App www.zoom-app.de

Fördert individuell – passt zum Schulbuch

Optimal für den Einsatz im Unterricht mit Notting Hill Gate! Stärken erkennen, Defizite beheben. Online-Lernstandsdiagnose und Auswertung auf Basis der aktuellen Bildungsstandards. Individuell zusammengestellte Fördermaterialien.

www.diesterweg.de/diagnose

Materialien für Lehrkräfte

- Lehrerfassung zum Schülerband 978-3-425-13991-3
- Teacher's Manual 978-3-425-14801-4
- Vorschläge für Lernerfolgskontrollen mit CD-ROM 978-3-425-14841-0
- Workbook mit Lösungen und Audio-CD 978-3-425-14811-3
- Audio-CD für Lehrkräfte 978-3-425-14831-1
- DVD für Lehrkräfte 978-3-425-14821-2
- Kopiervorlagen 978-3-425-14851-9
- Materialien für projektorientierten Unterricht 978-3-425-14071-1
- Wortbildkarten 978-3-425-14901-1
- BiBox - Digitale Lehrermaterialien
  Einzellizenz WEB-425-14891
  Kollegiumslizenz WEB-425-14899
  DVD-ROM-Version 978-3-425-14055-1
- Interaktive Whiteboard-Software
  Einzellizenz 978-3-425-14871-7
  Schullizenz 978-3-425-14087-6
- Differenzierung & Inklusion digital 978-3-425-14861-8
- Lernsoftware Schullizenz 978-3-425-14881-6

Druck A[1] / Jahr 2016
Alle Drucke der Serie A sind im Unterricht parallel verwendbar.

Redaktion: lüra – Klemt & Mues GbR, Wuppertal
Illustrationen: Ulf Marckwort, Kassel
Umschlaggestaltung: blum design und kommunikation GmbH, Hamburg
Umschlagfoto: Dirk Schmitz/dsphotos.de
Layout: tiff.any GmbH, Berlin
Satz: Anna-Maria Klages, Wuppertal
Druck und Bindung: westermann druck GmbH, Braunschweig

ISBN 978-3-425-**13961**-6

So arbeitest du mit dem Klassenarbeitstrainer zu *Notting Hill Gate 1*

Tipp Lies die Tipp-Kästen zu jeder Aufgabe genau durch. Sie geben dir **Schritt-für-Schritt-Hinweise** zum Lösen der verschiedenen Aufgabenformate.

Vor jeder Aufgabe steht ein Kreis ◯. Nimm dir nach dem Bearbeiten der Aufgabe Zeit, den Kreis auszumalen.

● (grün) Das kannst du schon gut: Prima!

● (gelb) Das fällt dir noch schwer.
Tipp: Lies dir die passenden Inhalte im TB und im WB nochmals durch und wiederhole die Übung.

● (rot) Übe die Inhalte nochmals intensiv! Im TB findest du ab Seite 162 Grammatikerklärungen, ab Seite 185 Vokabellisten.

Vergiss nicht, deine Fortschritte immer in deinen Lernplan auf Seite 4 bis 5 einzutragen.

Diese Symbole kennst du bereits aus dem TB:

☆ leichte Aufgabe

☾ mittelschwere Aufgabe

☼ schwierige Aufgabe

Du kannst selbst entscheiden, mit welchem Schwierigkeitsgrad du beginnen möchtest. Du kannst zum Beispiel mit der ☆ Aufgabe anfangen und anschließend mit ☾ und ☼ intensiver üben. Trau dir ruhig auch schwierigere Übungen zu! Überprüfe deine Antworten mit dem Lösungsteil (ab Seite 131).

Jede Klassenarbeit beginnt mit Aufgaben zum **Hörverstehen**. Höre dazu die beiliegende CD. Als Hilfe findest du die Texte dazu im Anhang (Seite 148).

Lies jeden Text ganz genau und **unterstreiche** wichtige Informationen.

Schreibe einen Text. Vergiss nicht, deine **Antworttexte** sorgfältig zu **überprüfen**.

Wiederhole die **Vokabeln** gründlich und **regelmäßig**. Bei einigen Aufgaben werden dir neue Wörter in Fußnoten erklärt.

Wiederhole die wichtigen Grammatikregeln im TB ab Seite 162.

Übertrage nur die gefragten **Informationen** von einer Sprache in die andere.

Die **Sprechaufgaben** sind Einzel- und Partneraufgaben. Übe immer mit einem Partner (z. B. Eltern, Freunde)! Dein Partner kann dir **Rückmeldung** geben, ob dein Gesagtes richtig war und was du noch verbessern kannst. Du kannst dich aber auch aufnehmen und die Aufnahme einem Partner vorspielen.

! Übe vor jeder Klassenarbeit besonders die Aufgaben, die beim ersten Bearbeiten einen ● (rot) bekommen haben.

Tipps für die Klassenarbeit

Lies die **Arbeitsanweisungen** zu jeder Aufgabe ganz **genau durch**!
Wenn du trotz genauen Lesens eine Anweisung nicht verstehst, frage deine(n) Englischlehrer(in).

☑ Achte darauf, dass du **immer** eine Antwort ankreuzt! Wenn du gar nichts ankreuzt, bekommst du überhaupt keine Punkte. Aber selbst wenn du raten musst, hast du eine gute Chance, die richtige Antwort auszuwählen.

Viel Spaß beim Üben mit dem Klassenarbeitstrainer!

Inhalt und Lernplan

Plane die Arbeit mit dem Klassenarbeitstrainer und **überprüfe** deine Ergebnisse: Gleiche jeden Abschnitt, z. B. *Listening*, *Reading*, sorgfältig mit dem Lösungsheft ab. Trage ein, wann du die Seiten bearbeitet hast und notiere in der Ampel, wie dir die Übungen gelungen sind.

bearbeitet am

LISTENING

Tipp

Schritt 1 – **Vor dem ersten Hören:** Lies die Aufgabe(n).
Schritt 2 – **Beim ersten Hören:** Bearbeite die Aufgabe(n).
Schritt 3 – **Beim zweiten Hören:** Vervollständige und verbessere deine Antworten.

Meet Greg and Matilda

☆ **a) Read the sentence beginnings and endings. Listen to Greg. Tick ✓ the right sentence endings. Listen again and check your answers.**

Lies die Satzanfänge und Satzenden. Höre Greg zu. Setze ein Häkchen ✓ beim richtigen Satzende. Höre den Text noch einmal an und kontrolliere deine Antworten.

1. Greg's name is …
   - ☐ Watson.
   - ☐ Miller.
   - ☐ Collins.
2. Greg is …
   - ☐ ten.
   - ☐ five.
   - ☐ eight.
3. Greg has got …
   - ☐ a sister.
   - ☐ a brother.
   - ☐ a sister and a brother.
4. Greg loves …
   - ☐ basketball.
   - ☐ tennis.
   - ☐ football.

b) Read the words. Listen to Matilda. What does she like? What has she got? Tick ✓ the right boxes. Listen again and check your answers.

Lies die Wörter. Höre Matilda zu. Was mag sie gern? Was hat sie? Setze ein Häkchen ✓ beim richtigen Wort. Höre den Text noch einmal an und kontrolliere deine Antworten.

☐ brother and sister	☐ skateboard	☐ hamburgers	☐ garden
☐ tennis	☐ piano	☐ bike	☐ pet
☐ dancing	☐ guitar	☐ pizza	☐ swimming

Meet Balraj and Fiona

a) Listen to the two children talking. Tick ✓ the right names. Sometimes you can tick more than one answer.

Höre den beiden Kindern zu. Setze ein Häkchen ✓ bei den richtigen Namen. Manchmal sind mehrere Antworten richtig.

	Balraj	Fiona
1. Who is from London?		
2. Whose parents are from India?		
3. Whose father lives in Birmingham?		
4. Who is twelve?		
5. Who has got a sister?		
6. Who has got a cat?		
7. Who plays football?		
8. Who loves music?		

b) Choose one child: Balraj or Fiona.
Then listen again and write down facts about him/her.

Wähle ein Kind aus: Balraj oder Fiona. Höre dann den Text noch einmal an und schreibe Informationen über das Kind auf.

name? ______

age? ______

brothers or sisters? ______

______

town? ______

hobbies? ______

______

______

______

READING

Tipp

Schritt 1 – **Vor dem Lesen:** Sieh dir die **Überschrift** an und überlege, worum es gehen könnte. Lies die Aufgabe(n) und überlege, was gesucht ist.

Schritt 2 – **Beim Lesen: Unterstreiche** die gesuchten Informationen.

http://kennyhooverthedog.worldpress.com

Woof, I'm Kenny Hoover and I'm three years old. I live in Hendon. That's in London. I've got a family: David Williams and his parents. They're very, very nice.

We live in a big house with a lovely garden. I love to sleep in the garden when the weather is nice, but I stay in the house when it rains. My best friend is Skipper and she is very friendly. We often go to the park together. Her family and my family are friends and Mrs. Williams and Mrs. Miller like to talk. When David and I go to the park, we always play with a ball. That's a lot of fun! It is my favourite hobby!

David always gives me my dog food. My favourite food is "Woof!". My dog bed is very big, but I love to sleep in David's bed. David loves it, too.

Kenny's blog

a) Read these sentences. Then read Kenny's blog. Tick ✓ right or wrong.

Lies die Aussagen. Dann lies Kennys Blog. Setze ein Häkchen ✓ für richtig oder falsch.

	right	wrong
1. Kenny Hoover is six years old.	☐	☐
2. Kenny Hoover lives with David and David's parents.	☐	☐
3. Kenny Hoover stays in the house when it rains.	☐	☐
4. Kenny Hoover's best friend is Barker.	☐	☐
5. Kenny Hoover loves to sleep in his dog bed.	☐	☐
6. Kenny Hoover's favourite food is "Woof!".	☐	☐

b) Read Kenny's blog. Write down facts about Kenny.

Lies Kennys Blog. Schreibe Informationen über ihn auf.

name:		age:	
town:		best friend:	
family:			
favourite hobby:			

WRITING

Tipp

Schritt 1 – **Vor dem Schreiben:** Prüfe, ob der Text eine bestimmte Form haben muss (z. B. E-Mail). Lege den Inhalt und die Reihenfolge fest.
Schritt 2 – **Schreibe** deinen Text.
Schritt 2 – **Überarbeite** deinen Text: Kontrolliere zuerst, ob alle Inhalte vorkommen. Prüfe dann, ob es grammatische Fehler gibt. Verbessere sie.

This is me

☆ **a) Write down facts about yourself.**

Schreibe Informationen über dich auf.

name:			
town:		age:	
family:			
hobby:			
best friend:			
favourite food:			

b) Use the information from a) to write a text about yourself. Write one sentence about each fact.

Verwende die Notizen aus a), um einen Text über dich zu schreiben. Schreibe zu jeder Information einen Satz.

My name ______ I am from ______ ______.
______ years old. My parents are ______
and I have got ______
I like to ______ in my
free time. My best friend ______
My favourite food ______
______
______

Hi, I'm Rajiv

name:	**Rajiv Patel**
town:	London, Notting Hill
age:	12
family:	parents from India, sister Sheree
languages:	English, Hindi
hobby:	cooking, playing the guitar
pet:	parrot called Ruby
best friends:	Gillian and Karla

Rajiv wants to write a blog about himself. Write his first text. Use the information from the grid. Write about 40 words.

Rajiv möchte einen Blog über sich schreiben. Schreibe seinen ersten Eintrag. Verwende die Informationen aus der Tabelle. Schreibe etwa 40 Wörter.

Hi, my name is

Welcome to Notting Hill

a) Collect information about Notting Hill. Use TB B1 (p. 28).

Sammle Informationen über Notting Hill. Schau im TB bei B1 (S. 28).

Notting Hill

sights:

activities:

places:

how to get there:

b) Use the information from a) to write a text about Notting Hill. Write about 50–60 words.

Verwende die Informationen aus a), um einen Text über Notting Hill zu schreiben. Schreibe ungefähr 50–60 Wörter.

WORDS AND GRAMMAR

Pets

Write the words under the pictures.

Schreibe die Wörter unter die passenden Bilder.

Tipp

Streiche die Begriffe, die du bereits verwendet hast, in der Box **durch**. So behältst du leichter den Überblick.

cat • mouse • parrot • dog • goldfish • rabbit

Weather words

Complete the sentences.

Vervollständige die Sätze.

1. In April there is a lot of ____________

2. In summer it is very ____________

3. The ____________ shines a lot in July.

4. You can fly a kite when it is ____________

5. May is in ____________

6. In winter we can build a ____________

People and places

Read the phrases. What do they describe? Find the right words.

Lies die Ausdrücke. Was beschreiben sie? Finde die richtigen Wörter.

1. Mum and dad: ______
2. Your aunt's/uncle's child: ______
3. A person who you like: ______
4. A person who lives next to you: ______
5. The day after Monday: ______

Pets and food

a) Complete the word webs. There are four more words than you need.

Vervollständige die Wortnetze. Es gibt vier Wörter mehr, als du benötigst.

Tipp

Streiche die Begriffe, die du bereits verwendet hast, in der Box **durch**. So behältst du leichter den Überblick.

pets | food

parrot • cat • market • tomato • park • rabbit • ice cream
playground • banana • cheese • hamster • swimming pool

b) Find two more words for each word web and add them.

Finde zwei weitere Wörter für jedes Wortnetz und ergänze sie.

c) Write the other words into the empty wordweb. Find a name for the word web.

Schreibe die übrigen Wörter in das leere Wortnetz. Finde einen Namen für das Wortnetz.

Phrases

a) **Match the parts of the phrases.**

Ordne die Ausdrücke einander zu.

Tipp

Schritt 1 – **Lies** erst alle Ausdrücke.
Schritt 2 – **Verbinde** die Ausdrücke zunächst ganz dünn mit Bleistift. Beginne mit den Ausdrücken, bei denen du dir ganz sicher bist.
Schritt 3 – **Prüfe**, ob alles passt.
Tipp: Vergiss nicht, die Nummern zum Schluss in die Tabelle einzutragen!

A	listen
B	meet
C	play
D	work
E	like
F	eat

1	the guitar
2	orange juice
3	with a partner
4	to the song
5	an apple
6	your friends

A	
B	
C	
D	
E	
F	

b) **Complete the phrases with words from the box.**

Vervollständige die Ausdrücke mit Wörtern aus dem Kasten.

Tipp

Streiche die Begriffe, die du bereits verwendet hast, in der Box **durch**. So behältst du leichter den Überblick.

speak • listen • play • talk • a T-shirt
the picture • a couch • the swimming pool

1. ______________ to music
2. ______________ to your partner
3. ______________ tennis
4. ______________ English
5. look at ______________
6. go to ______________
7. wear ______________
8. sit on ______________

c) **Find words to complete the phrases.**

Finde Wörter, die die Ausdrücke vervollständigen.

1. ______________________________ football

2. ________________________ your own chant

3. _________________________________ a pet

4. _____________________________ in a room

5. tell ___________________________________

6. like ___________________________________

7. ride ___________________________________

8. swim __________________________________

Gillian and David

Tipp

Überlege zuerst, ob es sich um den **Singular** (Einzahl) oder den **Plural** (Mehrzahl) handelt. Verwende beim **Plural** immer **‚are'** / **‚aren't'**!

Circle the right verb form.

Kreise die richtige Verbform ein.

Example: Gillian (is) / are twelve.

1. Gillian is / are David's cousin.
2. They is / are friends.
3. Gillian has got a cat. Her name is / are Butterfly.
4. David's pet isn't / aren't a cat.
5. It is / are a dog.
6. His name is / are Kenny Hoover.
7. David says: "I am / are eleven."
8. David's favourite sport isn't / am not basketball.
9. Gillian says: "I am / is from Notting Hill."
10. David says: "I am not / isn't from Notting Hill. I am / is from Hendon."
11. Gillian's favourite colour is / are red.

Rajiv and Karla

a) Complete the table. Use the right forms of 'to be'.

Vervollständige die Tabelle. Setze die richtigen Verbformen von „to be" ein.

are • is • am not • 're • are not • is not • aren't • 'm not • isn't • 'm • am • 's

	long form		short form	
	+	–	+	–
I				
you				
he / she / it				
we				
you				
they				

b) Fill in the right verb forms. The table in a) can help you.

Setze die richtigen Verbformen ein. Die Tabelle aus a) kann dir helfen.

1. Rajiv ______________________ twelve.
2. His parents ______________________ from India.
3. Rajiv says: "I ______________________ from Notting Hill."
4. Rajiv's best friends ______________________ Gillian and Karla.
5. His pet ______________________ a dog, it's a parrot.
6. Karla ______________________ Rajiv's friend.
7. They say: "We ______________________ from York, we ______________________ from London."

8. Karla's hobby ____________________ football – it ____________________ wheelchair basketball.

9. Karla says: "I ____________________ good at wheelchair basketball."
10. She ____________________ happy about that.
11. Karla's pet ____________________ a rabbit. His name is Hoppity.

◯ Vanessa

Fill in the right verb forms of 'to be'.

Setze die richtigen Verbformen von „to be" in die Lücken ein.

1. Vanessa is ____________________ from Hendon – she ____________________ from Notting Hill.
2. She ____________________ eleven.
3. Her parents ____________________ Dan and Janet.
4. They ____________________ from India.
5. Vanessa says: "I ____________________ in a football team, but I ____________________ in a basketball team."
6. "We ____________________ really good."
7. She asks: "What about you? ____________________ you in a football team?"
8. Vanessa's hobbies ____________________ also music and dancing.
9. Kenny Hoover ____________________ Vanessa's pet.
10. Vanessa has not got brothers or sisters. She ____________________ an only child[1].
11. Vanessa's hair ____________________ red.

1 *only child* ['əʊnli tʃaild]: Einzelkind

What have they got?

Megan	✗	✓	✓	✗	✗
Leo	✓	✗	✗	✓	✗
Mark	✓	✗	✓	✗	✓
Priya	✓	✓	✗	✗	✓

1 a) Answer the questions.

Beantworte die Fragen.

1. Who has got a computer? Megan, Priya
2. Who hasn't got a bike? ____________________
3. Who has got a skateboard? ____________________
4. Who hasn't got a rabbit? ____________________

1 b) Complete the sentences. Use the verb forms from the box.

Vervollständige die Sätze. Verwende die Verbformen aus dem Kasten.

have got • has got • haven't got • hasn't got

1. Leo and Mark ____________________ a computer.
2. Mark and Priya ____________________ a rabbit.
3. Megan says: "I ____________________ a parrot."
4. Leo ____________________ a parrot, but he ____________________ a rabbit.
5. Leo and Priya ____________________ bikes, but they ____________________ skateboards.
6. Mark ____________________ a bike, but he ____________________ a parrot.

1 c) Complete the questions. Use "Who has got" or "Who hasn't got".

Vervollständige die Fragen. Verwende "Who has got" or "Who hasn't got".

1. ______________________ a computer? – Leo and Mark.
2. ______________________ a rabbit? – Mark and Priya.
3. ______________________ a parrot? – Megan, Mark and Priya.
4. ______________________ a skateboard? – Priya and Leo.
5. ______________________ a bike? – Megan.

2 a) Write five sentences about what the children have or haven't got.

Schreibe fünf Sätze über das, was die Kinder haben oder nicht haben.

Priya ______________ a skateboard, but she ______________

2 b) Ask five questions about what the children have got and answer them.

Stelle fünf Fragen über das, was die Kinder haben, und beantworte diese.

Who ______________ a parrot? – ______________

–

–

–

–

Welcome to Notting Hill

a) Look at the picture. Then complete the sentences.

Schau dir das Bild an. Vervollständige dann die Sätze.

there is • there are

1. ______________________ a bus.
2. ______________________ children.
3. ______________________ three shops.
4. ______________________ a cat.

b) Answer the questions. Use short answers.

Beantworte die Fragen. Verwende Kurzantworten.

1. Is there a pet shop? – ______________________
2. Are there people with cars? – ______________________
3. Is there a park? – ______________________
4. Are there horses? – ______________________

c) Look at the picture. Write five sentences about what you see. Use the words and phrases from the box.

Schau dir das Bild an. Schreibe fünf Sätze über das, was du siehst. Verwende die Wörter und Ausdrücke aus dem Kasten.

restaurant • cars • pets • woman on a bike • parrot

1. ______________________________
2. ______________________________
3. ______________________________
4. ______________________________
5. ______________________________

d) Write questions about the picture and answer them with short answers. Use the words and phrases from the box.

Schreibe Fragen über das Bild auf und beantworte sie mit Kurzantworten. Verwende die Wörter und Ausdrücke aus dem Kasten.

museum • swimming pool • shops • man with a guitar • woman in a pink dress

1. ______________________________?
   ______________________________.
2. ______________________________?
   ______________________________.
3. ______________________________?
   ______________________________.
4. ______________________________?
   ______________________________.
5. ______________________________?
   ______________________________.

MEDIATION

Tipp

Gib in deinen eigenen Worten die **wichtigen Informationen** in der jeweils anderen Sprache wieder. Du musst **nicht Wort für Wort** übersetzen!

○ At the park

☆ **You are in England with your family. There, you meet other children. Help your little sister talk to them. Put the sentences in the correct order.**

Du bist mit deiner Familie in England. Dort trefft ihr andere Kinder. Hilf deiner kleinen Schwester, mit ihnen zu sprechen. Bringe die Sätze in die richtige Reihenfolge.

A	Where are you from?
B	Sehr gern! Sag ihnen das.
C	Do you like to play football?
D	Sie möchten wissen, wo wir herkommen.
E	We are from Germany.
F	Sag, dass wir aus Deutschland sind.
G	Sie möchten wissen, ob wir gern Fußball spielen.
H	OK, let's play.
I	Yes, very much!
J	Hello!

1	
2	
3	
4	
5	
6	
7	
8	
9	
10	

○ Say it in English, please!

☾ **You are in England with your family. You meet other children.**

Du bist mit deiner Familie in England. Ihr trefft andere Kinder.

Was sagst du auf Englisch, ...

1. ... wenn du sagen möchtest, wie alt du bist?

____

2. ... wenn du sagen möchtest, dass du eine Katze hast?

____

3. ... wenn du fragen möchtest, ob jemand einen Bruder hast?

____

4. … wenn du sagen möchtest, dass du Gitarre spielst?

____

5. … wenn du fragen möchtest, wo der Holland Park ist?

____

6. … wenn du fragen möchtest, ob jemand aus Notting Hill kommt?

____

Miles

You are in England with your family. You see this poster. Answer your brother's questions about it.

Du bist mit deiner Familie in England und siehst dieses Poster. Beantworte die Fragen deines Bruders.

Dein Bruder: Warum hängt das Plakat hier?

Du: ______________________________

____

Dein Bruder: Was steht denn da über die Katze?

Du: ______________________________

____

____

Dein Bruder: Und was machen wir, wenn wir sie sehen?

Du: ______________________________

____

____

LOST[1] CAT

"Miles"

Miles is seven years old.
He is black and white.
Miles is very friendly and always hungry. He likes to chase mice.
He lives at 65 Aubrey Road, Kensington, London.

We miss him a lot!

If you see him, please phone 0364 90 326, day or night.

1 *lost* [lɔst]: hier: entlaufen

SPEAKING

◯ Talking about places (ab Ende Theme 1)

☆ ☾ ☼ **Look at the picture and answer the questions.**

Schau dir das Bild an und beantworte die Fragen.

1. Where is Rajiv's parrot?
2. What can you buy at the "Retro" shop?
3. What is Rajiv's neighbour doing?
4. What is the new show called?

☆ **What can you see in the picture? Describe the area. The words in the box help you.**

Was kannst du auf dem Bild sehen? Beschreibe die Gegend. Die Wörter im Kasten helfen dir.

There is … • There are … • I can see ... • In the middle of[1] the street there are …

☾ **What can you see in the picture? Describe the area.**

Was kannst du auf dem Bild sehen? Beschreibe die Gegend.

☼ **What can you see in the picture? Describe the area and compare it to your area.**

Was kannst du auf dem Bild sehen? Beschreibe die Gegend und vergleiche sie mit deiner Gegend.

1 *in the middle of* [ɪn ðə ˈmɪdl ɔv]: in der Mitte von

LISTENING

Tipp

Schritt 1 – **Vor dem ersten Hören:** Lies die Aufgabe(n).
Schritt 2 – **Beim ersten Hören:** Bearbeite die Aufgabe(n).
Schritt 3 – **Beim zweiten Hören:** Vervollständige und verbessere deine Antworten.

Breakfast at school

☆ **Emma, Kelly, James and Omar want to have breakfast at school together. What kind of breakfast do the children want to have? Tick ✓ the correct answer.**

Emma, Kelly, James und Omar möchten in der Schule gemeinsam frühstücken. Welche Art Frühstück möchten die Kinder zubereiten? Setze ein Häkchen ✓ bei der richtigen Antwort.

☐ A big Sunday breakfast

☐ A schoolday breakfast

☐ A healthy breakfast

☆ **What do they need for their breakfast? Listen to the dialogue again and tick ✓ the correct pictures.**

Was brauchen sie für ihr Frühstück? Höre dir das Gespräch erneut an und setze ein Häkchen ✓ bei den richtigen Bildern.

1. ☐ 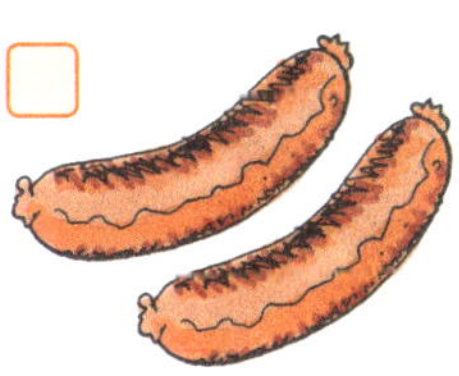

2. ☐ 

3. ☐ 

4. ☐ 

5. ☐ 

6. ☐ 

7. ☐ 

8. ☐ 

9. ☐ 

Who brings what? Listen and tick ✓ the correct name. Watch out: Some things are not brought by anyone.

Wer bringt was mit? Höre den Dialog an und setze ein Häckchen ✓ beim richtigen Kind. Gib acht: Manche Sachen werden von niemandem mitgebracht!

food and drink	Emma	Kelly	James	Omar
eggs				
sausages				
apples				
bananas				
tea				
muesli				
milk				
cake				
orange juice				

Listen to the dialogue again and answer the questions.

Höre den Text erneut an und beantworte die Fragen.

1. Who wants a Sunday breakfast?

____

____

2. Why don't the children have sausages?

____

____

3. Why don't the children have fried eggs?

____

____

____

READING

Tipp

Schritt 1 – **Vor dem Lesen:** Sieh dir die **Überschrift** an und überlege, worum es gehen könnte. Lies die Aufgabe(n) und überlege, was gesucht ist.

Schritt 2 – **Beim Lesen: Unterstreiche** die Informationen, die für die Aufgabe(n) gesucht werden.

Who is who?

A B C D

1. Peter is young, but very tall and slim. He has got short brown hair and a long nose. His clothes are blue.

2. Martha has short curly hair. She is not very slim. Her clothes are yellow and blue.

3. Walter is very old. He has got no hair and he wears glasses. He is not very tall. His clothes are red and grey.

4. Janet is small. Her hair is long and blonde. Her clothes are red and her shoes are white.

Read the texts and match the numbers to the correct letters.

Lies die Beschreibungen und ordne die Zahlen den richtigen Buchstaben zu.

A	B	C	D

Read these sentences. Tick ✓ right or wrong.

Lies die Sätze. Setze ein Häkchen ✓ bei richtig oder falsch.

	right	wrong
1. Walter is tall.	☐	☐
2. Peter has got black hair.	☐	☐
3. Janet's clothes are red.	☐	☐
4. Martha has got curly hair.	☐	☐

Read these sentences. Answer the questions.

Lies die Sätze. Beantworte die Fragen.

1. What colour are Walter's clothes?

___

___

2. Who has got blonde hair?

___

___

3. What can you say about Peter's nose?

___

___

4. Who is very tall and slim?

___

___

Hendon School News

Read the Hendon School News.

Lies die Neuigkeiten aus der Hendon School.

Hendon School News

What do our teachers and pupils do at the weekends?

Mrs Lamont:
I like to play the piano at the weekend. I also go to the theatre very often. And I meet my friends. We like to have dinner at a nice restaurant.

Laura Scott (7RK):
I play football every Saturday. After that I do my homework. On Sundays I stay in bed all morning. Then I get up and walk the dog.

Mr Kapoor:
On Sundays I always get up early. Then I go for a run in the park. After that I have breakfast with my family. In the afternoon we go to the swimming pool.

James Liu (8ML):
I like to read at the weekend. I also listen to music, play the guitar or play computer games. On Saturdays I go swimming with my dad.

☆ **Look at the pictures. Who does what? Write the names under the pictures.**

Schau dir die Bilder an. Wer macht was? Schreibe die Namen unter die Bilder.

1. ______________________

2. ______________________

3. ______________________

4. ______________________

Tick ☑ the right names. Sometimes you can tick more than one name.

Setze ein Häkchen ☑ unter den richtigen Namen. Manchmal sind mehrere Antworten richtig.

	Mrs Lamont	Laura Scott	Mr Kapoor	James Liu
1. Who meets friends?				
2. Who walks the dog?				
3. Who plays an instrument?				
4. Who does sport?				
5. Who goes to the swimming pool?				
6. Who likes to read?				
7. Who likes to go to the theatre?				
8. Who does his/her homework?				
9. Who eats at a restaurant?				
10. Who likes to spend all morning in bed?				

WRITING

Tipp

Schritt 1 – **Vor dem Schreiben:** Prüfe, ob der Text eine bestimmte Form haben muss (z. B. E-Mail). Lege den Inhalt und die Reihenfolge fest.
Schritt 2 – **Schreibe** deinen Text.
Schritt 3 – **Überarbeite** deinen Text: Kontrolliere zuerst, ob alle Inhalte vorkommen. Prüfe dann, ob es grammatische Fehler gibt. Verbessere sie.

☆ Jonah's Saturday

Write a text about Jonah and what he does on Saturdays. The words and phrases from the boxes can help you. Write about 40 words.

Schreibe einen Text über Jonah und über das, was er samstags macht. Die Ausdrücke und Wörter aus den Kästchen helfen dir dabei. Schreibe ungefähr 40 Wörter.

Every Saturday ... On Saturdays ... Each Saturday morning ... First, ... Then, ... After that, ...	Jonah he	get up • read a book • go to school • play basketball • meet friends • walk the dog • do homework • watch TV • go to bed

Start like this: On **Saturdays** Jonah **doesn't play** tennis. He **goes** to the swimming pool with his friends.

On Saturdays Jonah

◯ ☾ Anaya's Sunday

Write a text about Anaya and what she does on Sundays. Use the ideas from the box. Add details if you like. Write about 50 words.

Schreibe einen Text über Anaya und darüber, was sie sonntags macht. Benutze die Ideen aus dem Kasten. Du kannst Details hinzufügen. Schreibe ungefähr 50 Wörter.

get up • play tennis • meet friends • play with the cat • have dinner

Start like this: On Sundays Anaya **has** breakfast at 8:30.

On Sundays Anaya ______________________________

____

____

____

____

____

◯ ☼ Your turn: At the weekend

Write a text about yourself and what you do at weekends. List ideas before you start. Write about 60 words.

Schreibe einen Text über dich selbst und darüber, was du an den Wochenenden machst. Sammle Ideen, bevor du anfängst. Schreibe ungefähr 60 Wörter.

- get up
- ______
- ______
- ______
- ______
- ______
- ______
- ______
- ______

On Saturdays I always ______________________________

____

____

____

____

____

____

WORDS AND GRAMMAR

Word lists

Tipp

Schritt 1 – **Lies** erst alle Ausdrücke.
Schritt 2 – **Ordne** die Ausdrücke zu. Beginne mit den Ausdrücken, bei denen du dir ganz sicher bist.
Schritt 3 – **Prüfe**, ob alles passt.

face • muesli • ruler • parents • chalk • neck • cornflakes • classmate • leg • back • toast • friend • schoolbag • bacon • jam • sister • tooth • pencil case • exercise book • neighbour • fried egg • pen • tummy • teacher

school things	body parts	breakfast things	

Write the words in the right white lists. There are six words for each list. Watch out: There are more words than you need.

Schreibe die Wörter in die richtigen weißen Spalten. Jede Liste muss sechs Wörter enthalten. Gib acht: Es gibt mehr Wörter, als du benötigst.

Find six more words.

Ergänze insgesamt sechs weitere Wörter.

Write the other words in the grey list. Find a name for this list.

Schreibe die übrigen Wörter in die graue Spalte. Finde einen Überbegriff für diese Spalte.

Add one word to the grey list.

Ergänze ein Wort in der grauen Spalte.

◯ The clock is ticking …

☆ ☾ ☼ **Draw the hands[1] on the clocks.**

Zeichne die Zeiger in die Uhren ein.

Tipp

Anders als im Deutschen gibt man im Englischen nicht die halbe Stunde **VOR** der vollen Stunde an, sondern die **NACH** der vollen Stunde. 'Halb vier' heißt also *‚half past three'*.

It's ten to three.

It's half past twelve.

It's twenty past nine.

It's quarter to five.

☾ ☼ **Write down the times in two different ways.**

Schreibe die Uhrzeiten auf zwei verschiedene Arten auf.

It's ______________________ It's ______________________

It's ______________________ It's ______________________

It's ______________________ It's ______________________

☼ **When do YOU do things? Complete the clock/watch and write down the times.**

Wann machst DU bestimmte Dinge? Vervollständige die Uhren und trage die Zeiten ein.

I have breakfast at ______________________

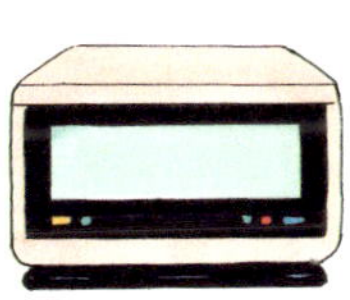

I finish school at ______________________

1 *hand* [hænd]: Zeiger

In the classroom

What does Mr Dixon tell the pupils? Match the sentence parts and write down the correct numbers in the boxes.

Was bittet Mr Dixon seine Schüler zu tun? Finde heraus, welche Satzteile zueinander passen, und schreibe rechts die richtigen Ziffern auf.

Tipp

Schritt 1 – **Lies** erst alle Ausdrücke.
Schritt 2 – **Verbinde** die Ausdrücke zunächst ganz dünn mit Bleistift. Beginne mit den Ausdrücken, bei denen du dir ganz sicher bist.
Schritt 3 – **Prüfe**, ob alles passt.
Tipp: Vergiss nicht, die Nummern am Ende in die Tabelle einzutragen!

A	Close
B	Answer
C	Don't
D	Make
E	Act
F	Sit
G	Stop
H	Work

1	play with your rubber.
2	talking now.
3	down, please.
4	the question.
5	your own dialogue.
6	in pairs.
7	out the scene.
8	the door, please!

A	
B	
C	
D	
E	
F	
G	
H	

What does Mr Dixon tell the pupils to do? Find words and complete the sentences.

Was bittet Mr Dixon seine Schüler zu tun? Finde passende Wörter und vervollständige die Sätze.

1. ______________________ at the picture.
2. ______________________ to the CD.
3. ______________________ to your partner about the task.
4. ______________________ in groups of four.
5. ______________________ down the answer.
6. ______________________ to page 23.
7. ______________________ the window, please.
8. ______________________ quiet, please!

What does Mr Dixon tell the pupils NOT to do? Make three sentences and write them down.

Was bittet Mr Dixon seine Schüler, NICHT zu tun? Bilde drei Sätze und schreibe sie auf.

Don't	talk forget walk	your homework around to your neighbour

School rules

a) Look at the phrases in the box. Make a poster with school rules that tells pupils what (not) to do.

Schau dir die Ausdrücke in den Kästen an. Erstelle ein Poster mit Schulregeln, das den Schülern sagt, was sie (nicht) machen sollen.

✓	be nice do your homework listen to the teachers wear the school uniform	×	be late use mobiles at school eat during lessons play football in the classroom

School Rules

b) Find two more (useful!) rules. Add them to the list.

Finde zwei weitere (sinnvolle!) Regeln. Füge sie der Liste hinzu.

The Millers' morning

Complete the sentences. Use the verbs from the box.

Vervollständige die Sätze. Benutze die Verben aus dem Kasten.

Tipp

Streiche die Verbformen, die du bereits verwendet hast, in der Box **durch**. So behältst du leichter den Überblick.

makes • go • have • tells • goes • ~~go to bed~~ • get up • brushes

Example: Mr and Mrs Miller ___go to bed___ at 11 o'clock.

1. Mr and Mrs Miller ______________ at 6:45 in the morning.
2. Mr Miller ______________ breakfast.
3. Mrs Miller ______________ the children to get up.
4. They all ______________ breakfast at 7:15 in the morning.
5. Ben ______________ his teeth at 7:45 in the morning.
6. The children ______________ to school at 8:15 in the morning.
7. Mrs Miller ______________ to work at 8:20 in the morning.

The Lees' morning

Circle the right verb form.

Kreise das richtige Verb ein.

Example: Mr and Mrs Lee gets / (get) up at 7 o'clock.

1. Yung gets / get up at 7 o'clock, too.
2. Then he goes / go to the bathroom.
3. His sisters gets / get up at 7:10 in the morning.
4. Yung and his mother makes / make breakfast at 7:15 in the morning.
5. They has / have breakfast at 7:30 in the morning.
6. Then the children brushes / brush their teeth.
7. Mr Lee goes / go to work at 8 o'clock.
8. Yung and his sisters leaves / leave the house at 8:15 in the morning.

The Jarvies' morning

a) **Complete the sentences. Use the verbs from the box. Put them into the correct form.**

Vervollständige die Sätze. Verwende die Verben aus dem Kasten. Setze sie in die richtige Form.

make • go • have • play • get up • brush • get up • read • leave • wash

1. Mr and Mrs Jarvie ______________________________ at 7 o'clock.
2. Mrs Jarvie ______________________________ breakfast.
3. Mr Jarvie ______________________________ with the dog.
4. Sam ______________________________ up at 7:15 in the morning.
5. They all ______________________________ breakfast at 7:45 in the morning.
6. Sam ______________________________ his face and ______________________________ his hair at 8 o'clock.

7. He also ______________________________ a comic.
8. Then he ______________________________ to school.
9. His parents ______________________________ the house at 8:30 in the morning.

b) **Why do you have to use different verb forms? Explain the rule.**

Warum musst du unterschiedliche Verbformen verwenden? Erkläre die Regel.

Tipp

Schritt 1 – **Überlege**, warum und wann du unterschiedliche Formen verwendest.
Schritt 2 – Mache dir **stichwortartig Notizen**.
Schritt 3 – Schreibe die Regel **sauber auf**.

____

____

____

____

____

____

Friends from London

☆ **Match the questions and answers. Answer 'yes' ✓ or 'no' ✗ Write down the correct numbers in the boxes.**

Ordne die Antworten den Fragen zu. Bejahe ✓ oder verneine ✗ die Fragen. Schreibe rechts die richtigen Ziffern auf.

Tipp

Schritt 1 – **Lies** erst alle Ausdrücke.
Schritt 2 – **Verbinde** die Ausdrücke zunächst ganz dünn mit Bleistift. Beginne mit den Ausdrücken, bei denen du dir ganz sicher bist.
Schritt 3 – **Prüfe**, ob alles passt.
Tipp: Vergiss nicht, die Nummern am Ende in die Tabelle einzutragen!

A	Are Myra and Lily cousins? ✓	1	Yes, she does.		A	4
B	Does Vladik play an instrument? ✓	2	No, he isn't		B	
C	Does Emma like bacon? ✗	3	No, they aren't.		C	
D	Is Ian 14? ✗	4	Yes, they are.		D	
E	Does Hannah play football? ✓	5	Yes, he does.		E	
F	Do Vladik and Hannah live in York? ✗	6	Yes, he is.		F	
G	Are Lucy's parents from Germany? ✗	7	No, they don't.		G	
H	Is Adam eleven? ✓	8	No, she doesn't.		H	

☾ **Answer questions about the children. Answer 'yes' ✓ or 'no' ✗ .**

Beantworte die Fragen über die Kinder. Bejahe ✓ oder verneine ✗ die Fragen.

Example: Does Hannah play tennis? ✗ No, she doesn't.

1. Is Molly Myra's cat? ✗ ____________________
2. Are Myra and Lily friends? ✓ ____________________
3. Do Vladik and Hanah live in Hendon? ✓ ____________________
4. Are Emma and Abigail sisters? ✗ ____________________
5. Does Theodore love burgers? ✓ ____________________
6. Do Lucy and Adam love baseball? ✗ ____________________
7. Is Sharon Adam's sister? ✓ ____________________
8. Does Lily like tomatoes? ✗ ____________________

☼ **Make questions and give short answers. Answer 'yes' ✓ or 'no' ✗.**

Bilde Fragen und beantworte sie. Bejahe ✓ oder verneine ✗ die Fragen.

1. Ishan's parents • speak Hindi? ✓

   ______________________________ – ______________

2. Emily and Ishan • friends? ✓

   ______________________________ – ______________

3. Baxter • Olivia's dog? ✗

   ______________________________ – ______________

4. Chloe • like music? ✓

   ______________________________ – ______________

5. Ahmed • a bad cook? ✗

   ______________________________ – ______________

6. Olivia • play football? ✓

   ______________________________ – ______________

'A' or 'an'

☆ **Add 'a' or 'an'.**

Ergänze 'a' oder 'an'.

___ dog   ___ animal   ___ friend   ___ answer   ___ car

___ idea   classroom   ___ elephant   ___ teacher   ___ pet

☾ **Add 'a' or 'an'.**

Ergänze 'a' oder 'an'.

___ open door   ___ window   ___ old desk   ___ table

___ great idea   ___ interesting book   ___ extra task   ___ blue exercise book

___ clever answer   ___ egg   ___ English breakfast

___ old overhead projector   ___ orange scarf

When do you use 'a', and when do you use 'an'? Explain the difference.

Wann verwendest du 'a', wann verwendest du 'an'? Erkläre den Unterschied.

______

______

______

______

______

Add 'a' or 'an'.

Ergänze 'a' oder 'an'.

1. Is this ______ English book? – No, it's ______ German book.
2. I have cornflakes and ______ apple for breakfast.
3. This isn't ______ new pencil. It's ______ old pencil.
4. Is this ______ exercise book? – Oh no, it's ______ textbook.
5. I have ______ great idea!
6. Do you have ______ answer for this question?
7. In school, we read ______ interesting book.

Add 'a' or 'an'. Explain why you use 'a' or 'an' in these examples.

Erkläre, warum man in diesen Beispielen 'a' oder 'an' verwendet.

an uncle /'ʌŋkl/	but	a uniform /'ju:nɪfɔ:m/
a hobby /'hɔbi/	but	an hour /aʊə/

______

______

______

______

______

MEDIATION

Tipp

Gib mit eigenen Worten die **wichtigen Informationen** in der jeweils **anderen Sprache** wieder. Du musst **nicht Wort für Wort** übersetzen!

Breakfast at a restaurant

You and your family are on a holiday trip to Great Britain, but your parents and your brother do not speak English. Help them choose their breakfast at a restaurant. Choose ☆, ☾ or ☼.

Du bist mit deiner Familie im Urlaub in Großbritannien, aber die anderen sprechen kein Englisch. Hilf ihnen, im Restaurant ein Frühstück auszusuchen. Wähle ☆, ☾ oder ☼.

☆ Bruder: Ich möchte gern etwas trinken. Gibt es hier Saft?

Du: ______________________________

Bruder: Ich glaube, ich möchte doch lieber etwas Warmes. Gibt es hier heiße Milch?

Du: ______________________________

☾ Mutter: Kann man nur Kaffee oder auch Tee bestellen?

Du: ______________________________

Mutter: Ich würde gern etwas Gesundes essen. Steht da was auf der Karte?

Du: ______________________________

Mutter: Gibt es vielleicht auch Vollkornbrot?

Du: ______________________________

☼ Vater: Ich würde gern ein englisches Frühstück probieren! Was kann ich da bestellen?

Du: ______________________________

Vater: Gibt es auch noch Toast dazu?

Du: ______________________________

Vater: Und was ist mit Eiern? Kann ich ein Spiegelei bekommen?

Du: ______________________________

Vater: Hm, vielleicht nehme ich doch lieber Rührei. Gibt es das auch?

Du: ______________________________

Juices

Apple	£1.50
Orange	£2.00
Grapefruit	£2.00

Hot Drinks

Coffee	£1.50
Tea	£1.20
Milk	£1.20
Hot Chocolate	£1.80

Cold Drinks

Water	£1.00
Lemonade	£1.20
Coke	£1.20

Eggs

Boiled	£0.80
Scrambled	£2.50
Fried	£2.00

Toast & Muffins

Muffin	£1.50
Toast with butter	£1.00
Toast with jam	£1.30

English Breakfast

Bacon	£2.50
Sausage	£2.50
Baked beans	£1.50

In a Bowl

Cornflakes	£2.00
Muesli	£2.50
Porridge	£2.00

SPEAKING

On the way to school (ab Ende Theme 2)

Partner/-in A

Du nimmst an einem Schüleraustausch teil. Dein englischer Gastschüler/deine Gastschülerin begleitet dich zur Schule.

1 Frage Partner/-in B, wie spät es ist.

3 Bitte Partner/-in B sich zu beeilen, weil ihr spät dran seid.

5 Sage, dass die Schule um 8:10 Uhr beginnt.

7 Erwidere, dass du deine Hausaufgaben für Englisch hast.

Partner/-in B

Du nimmst als englischer Gastschüler an einem Schüleraustausch teil.
Du begleitest deinen Gastgeber/deine Gastgeberin zur Schule.

2 Sage, dass es 8:00 Uhr ist.

4 Frage, wann die Schule beginnt.

6 Frage, ob Partner/-in A seine/ihre Hausaufgaben für Englisch hat.

8 Sage, dass das gut ist.

☆ **Have a conversation. The words in the boxes help you.**

Führt eine Unterhaltung. Die Wörter in den Kästen helfen euch.

Partner/in A

What time ...? • Hurry ..., we're... • School starts ... • Yes, ...

Partner/in B

It's ... • When does ...? • Have you got ...? • That's ...

☾ **Have a conversation.**

Führt eine Unterhaltung.

Have a conversation.

Führt eine Unterhaltung.

Partner/-in A

In einem Schüleraustausch nimmst du deinen Gastschüler/deine Gastschülerin mit zur Schule.

1 Frage Partner/-in B, wie spät es ist.

3 Bitte Partner/-in B sich zu beeilen, weil ihr spät dran seid.

5 Sage, dass die Schule um 8:10 Uhr beginnt.

7 Erwidere, dass du deine Hausaufgaben für Englisch nicht hast.

9 Erkläre die Aufgabe: „Schreibe einen Text über dein Haustier".

11 Verneine und frage Partner/-in B, wie man auf Englisch „Ich habe kein Haustier" sagt.

Partner/-in B

Du bist der englische Gastschüler und begleitest deinen Gastgeber/deine Gastgeberin zur Schule.

2 Sage, dass es 8:00 Uhr ist.

4 Frage, wann die Schule beginnt.

6 Frage, ob Partner/-in A seine/ihre Hausaufgaben für Englisch hat.

8 Biete A Hilfe an. Frage, was die Hausaufgabe ist.

10 Frage Partner/-in A ob er/sie ein Haustier hat.

12 Erkläre, wie man auf Englisch „Ich habe kein Haustier" sagt.

Polly and Spot

Look at Polly the monster and describe her. The words in the box help you.

Sieh dir das Monster Polly an und beschreibe sie. Die Wörter im Kasten helfen dir.

Polly is … small • tall • She has got … • I can see …

Look at Polly the monster and describe her.

Sieh dir das Monster Polly an und beschreibe sie.

Look at the monsters Polly and Spot and describe them.

Sieh dir die Monster Polly und Spot an und beschreibe sie.

LISTENING

What can I do in my free time?

Tipp

Schritt 1 – **Vor dem ersten Hören:** Lies die Aufgabe(n).
Schritt 2 – **Beim ersten Hören:** Bearbeite die Aufgabe(n).
Schritt 3 – **Beim zweiten Hören:** Vervollständige und verbessere deine Antworten.

Listen to the dialogue. What are Eleanor and Jacob talking about? Tick ✓ the right answer.

Höre dir das Gespräch an. Worüber sprechen Eleanor und Jacob? Setze bei der richtigen Antwort ein Häkchen ✓ .

The conversation is about ...

☐ 

☐ 

☐ 

Listen again. Are the statements right or wrong? Tick ✓ the correct box.

Lies die Sätze. Setze ein Häkchen ✓ *bei richtig oder falsch.*	right	wrong
1. Jacob plays tennis on Thursdays.	☐	☐
2. Swimming starts at 4 o'clock.	☐	☐
3. On Friday football starts at 5 o'clock.	☐	☐
4. On Monday Jacob swims in the pool.	☐	☐
5. Hockey starts at 6 o'clock on Tuesday.	☐	☐
6. Jacob goes inline skating in the gym.	☐	☐

Listen to the dialogue. On what day and at what time does Jacob do which sport? Take notes in the grid below.

Höre dir das Gespräch an. Wann macht Jacob welche Sportart? Notiere in der Tabelle.

sport	swimming	hockey	tennis	inline skating	football
Monday When?					
Tuesday When?					
Wednesday When?					
Thursday When?					
Friday When?					

Listen to the dialogue. When and where does Jacob do which sport? Take short notes in the grid below.

Höre dir das Gespräch an. Wann und wo macht welchen Jacob Sport? Notiere Stichworte in der Tabelle.

activity	swimming	hockey	tennis	inline skating	football
Monday When? Where?					
Tuesday When? Where?					
Wednesday When? Where?					
Thursday When? Where?					
Friday When? Where?					

READING

An event

Tipp

Schritt 1 – **Vor dem Lesen:** Sieh dir die **Überschrift** an und überlege, worum es in dem Text gehen könnte. Lies die Aufgabe(n) und überlege, was gesucht ist.
Schritt 2 – **Beim Lesen: Unterstreiche** die Informationen, die für die Aufgabe(n) gesucht werden.
Schritt 3 – **Während des Lesens:** Unterstreiche beim Lesen die gesuchten Informationen.

Horseback riding!

When:	Friday to Sunday, August 16th to 18th Every day from 10 am to 6 pm
Where:	Playing field at Holland Park School
Who can come:	Anybody who likes horses!
What:	jumping and horse races[1]
Tickets:	£ 12 per person / day
Food:	pizza, popcorn, chocolate, sandwiches
Drinks:	lemonade, tea, coffee, water

1 race [reɪs]: Rennen

Look at the poster and answer the questions.

Sieh dir das Poster an und beantworte die Fragen.

1. What sport does the poster present? ______
2. On what days can you do this sport? ______
3. When does it start in the morning? ______
4. Where can you see the horses? ______
5. How much is a ticket? ______
6. What can you eat and drink there? ______

Pets

Read the following posters about different pets. Complete the sentences.

Lies die folgenden Poster über die Haustiere. Vervollständige die Sätze.

Fluffy is my guinea pig.
She lives in a small cage in my room. Her favourite food is spinach. Sometimes I take her out into the garden.

Blacky is my dog. He is nine years old and has four white feet. The rest of him is black. He eats dog food and bones and sleeps outside.
I take him for a walk every day.

Arthur is my chicken.
I live on a farm and feed the animals every day.
Arthur eats vegetables.
He and his brothers and sisters live in the barn[1].

The name of my cat is Tigger.
She is really big and loves to eat a lot. Tigger is yellow and black. She eats cat food and drinks milk.
She sleeps in a basket in my room.

Bronwen is my horse.
She is very tall and can run fast.She likes to jump and run around the field with other horses. She eats apples and carrots.

My parrot's name is Kiki.
She lives in a cage in my room.
She is white and has a yellow beak[2]. She eats fruit all day.
I talk to her all the time.

Mike: I live on a farm and my pet is a ______________________________.

Alex: My pet has a big yellow beak and is called ______________________________.

Lucy: I take my pet into the garden and she is a ______________________________.

Ross: My pet is big and likes carrots. She is a ______________________________.

Sarah: My pet is big and is called ______________________________.

Jane: My pet has four legs and white feet and he is a ______________________________.

1 *barn* [baːn]: Scheune   2 *beak* [biːk]: Schnabel

Read the sentences about the pets and correct them.

Lies die Sätze über die Haustiere und verbessere sie.

1. Tigger sleeps in a cage and eats cat food.

2. Bronwen is very tall and eats spinach.

3. Arthur eats bones and lives with his brother and sisters.

4. Fluffy lives in a small cage and eats cat food.

5. Kiki has a yellow beak and drinks milk.

6. Blacky sleeps outside and eats carrots.

7. Fluffy is nine years old and I take him for a walk every day.

WRITING

My (dream) pet

Tipp

Schritt 1 – **Vor dem Schreiben:** Prüfe, ob der Text eine bestimmte Form haben muss (z. B. E-Mail). Lege den Inhalt und die Reihenfolge fest.
Schritt 2 – **Schreibe** deinen Text.
Schritt 3 – **Überarbeite** deinen Text: Kontrolliere zuerst, ob alle Inhalte vorkommen. Prüfe dann, ob es grammatische Fehler gibt. Verbessere sie.

☆ **Write about your (dream) pet. The phrases and examples in the boxes can help you. Write about 50 words.**

Schreibe einen Text über dein (Traum-)Haustier. Die Satzanfänge in den Kästen helfen dir. Schreibe ungefähr 50 Wörter.

My favourite (dream) pet is ...
dog • cat • parrot • guinea pig • chicken • horse

It eats ...
apples • dog food • cat food • spinach • bones • carrots

It is ... years old. • It sleeps ...
in my room • in a basket • in a cage • in the garden • outside

I love it because ...
it is my best friend. • I play with him/her. • it can run fast. • it is very funny.

It can ...
speak • roll over • jump

I take it ...
to school • for a walk • to the vet[1] • to my friend's house • to the park • to the playground

It has ...
black • yellow • white • feet • eyes

1 *vet* [vɛt]: Tierarzt

My favourite (dream) pet is

It is   years old. It has

It eats

It sleeps

It can

I take it

I love it because

Write about your (dream) pet. The phrases and examples in the boxes help you. Write about 60 words.

Schreibe einen Text über dein (Traum-)Haustier. Die Satzanfänge und Beispiele in den Kästen helfen dir. Schreibe ungefähr 60 Wörter.

guinea pig • horse • chicken • parrot • black • yellow • apples • bones • carrots • spinach • in the garden • in a cage • for a walk • to the vet[1] • to the park • speak • roll over • jump

My favourite (dream) pet is ... | **It is ... years old.** | **It has ...** | **It eats ...** | **It sleeps ...** | **It can ...** | **I take it ...** | **I love it because ...**

1 *vet* [vɛt]: Tierarzt

☼ **Write about your (dream) pet. The phrases in the boxes help you. Write about 70 words.**

Schreibe einen Text über dein (Traum-) Haustier. Die Satzanfänge in den Kästen helfen dir. Schreibe ungefähr 70 Wörter.

My favourite (dream) pet is ... It is ... years old. It has ... It eats ... It sleeps ... It can ... I take it ... I love it because ...

An exotic pet

☼ **Look at the picture. Write about the pet. Find a good name for the animal. The phrases in the box help you. Write about 70 words.**

Schau dir das Bild an. Dann schreibe einen Text über das Haustier. Finde einen guten Namen für das Tier. Die Satzanfänge im Kasten helfen dir. Schreibe ungefähr 70 Wörter.

This is a(n) ... | **Its name is ...** | **It has ...** | **Its favourite food is ...** | **It can ...** | **It sleeps ...**

What can they do?

☆ ☾ **What can the children do? What can't they do? Look at the pictures and write the sentences down.**

Was können die Kinder und was können sie nicht? Sieh dir die Bilder an und schreibe die Sätze auf.

Example: The boy can't swim.

____

____

____

____

____

____

☼ **Now write about yourself. What can and what can't you do? Write 3 sentences with can and can't.**

Schreibe jetzt über dich selbst. Was kannst du und was nicht? Schreibe jeweils drei Sätze mit ‚can' und ‚can't'.

Example: I can swim but I can't play volleyball.

____

____

____

____

____

WORDS AND GRAMMAR

Types of sport

go • ride • do • play

Match the sports with a verb from the box.

Welches Verb passt zu welcher Sportart?

1. ______________________ swimming
2. ______________________ skating
3. ______________________ basketball
4. ______________________ a bike
5. ______________________ skiing
6. ______________________ hockey
7. ______________________ volleyball
8. ______________________ karate
9. ______________________ gymnastics
10. ______________________ football
11. ______________________ a horse
12. ______________________ table tennis

Write down phrases for the these sports.

Schreibe Ausdrücke zu den Sportarten auf.

go • ride • do • play

1. 
2. 
3. 
4. 
5. 
6. 
7. 
8. 
9. 
10. 
11. 
12. 

1. go swimming
2. ______________________
3. ______________________
4. ______________________
5. ______________________
6. ______________________
7. ______________________
8. ______________________
9. ______________________
10. ______________________
11. ______________________
12. ______________________

Where can you do which sport? Look at the example and write phrases.

Wo kann man diese Sportarten betreiben? Sieh dir das Beispiel an und schreibe Ausdrücke auf.

1. go swimming in a pool
2. ______________________
3. ______________________
4. ______________________
5. ______________________
6. ______________________
7. ______________________
8. ______________________
9. ______________________
10. ______________________
11. ______________________
12. ______________________

Odd one out

Circle the "odd one out". Put the five words that do not fit in the sentences below. Look at the example and do the other five.

Kreise die fünf unpassenden Wörter ein. Setze sie in die Sätze unten ein. Sieh dir das Beispiel an.

Example: listen • watch • (game) • help

1. sports hall • pool • sports field • library
2. what • winner • where • when
3. singer • teacher • goalkeeper • family
4. sticker • fantastic • postcard • mug
5. always • sometimes • usually • today

Example: I like watching a football game on TV.

The Holland Park team scores two goals and is the ______________ of the game.

David goes to the ______________ on Thursday to read books.

"Josh, I want you to take the rubbish out ______________, not tomorrow."

The match between Holland Park and Hendon was absolutely ______________.

We are a very active ______________. My dad is a runner, my mum plays volleyball and I ride a horse.

Matching 

a) **Match the opposites and write them down.**

Verbinde die Gegensätze und schreibe sie auf.

Tipp

Streiche die Wörter oder Wortteile, die du bereits verwendet hast, in der Box **durch**. So behältst du leichter den Überblick.

love can ask funny big seller easy am boy buy long new

small pm answer short can't old hate difficult girl boring sell customer

1. ______
2. ______
3. ______
4. ______
5. ______
6. ______
7. ______
8. ______
9. ______
10. ______
11. ______
12. ______

b) **Put these words together and write them down.**

Setze die Wörter zusammen und schreibe sie auf.

sea- foot- class- post- play- black- week- some- lunch- goal-

-ground -board -card -keeper -shell -time -ball -thing -mate -end

1. ______
2. ______
3. ______
4. ______
5. ______
6. ______
7. ______
8. ______
9. ______
10. ______

◯ Words, words, words …

☼ **Look at Theme 3 (vocabulary p. 209–218) and find:**

Sieh dir Theme 3 (Vokabeln S. 209–218) an und finde:

- two sports you can **do**.

____

____

- four **question** words.

____

____

- five words with "**ea**".

ready _______________

____

- five **adjectives**.

____

____

- five words with **double consonants** (e.g. ll, nn …):

____

____

- one word that **rhymes** with each of the following words:

classmate – _______________

see – _______________

game – _______________

will – _______________

play – _______________

◯ What can or can't they do?

☆ **Write down what these people can do and what they can't do.**

Schreibe auf, was die Personen können und was sie nicht können.

Example: Peter:

dance ✓ ride a bike ✗

Peter can dance but he can't ride a bike.

1. Sharon:

run fast ✗ swim ✓

Sharon can ______

but she can't ______

2. Josephine:

do gymnastics ✓ play basketball ✗

Josephine can ______

but she can't ______

3. Sheree:

do karate ✓ play hockey ✗

______

______

4. Hoppity:

eat carrots ✓ sleep in a basket ✗

______

______

5. Gillian and Vanessa:

collect stickers ✓ ride a horse ✗

______

______

6. David and Rajiv:

ride bike ✓ feed pets ✗

______

______

Write down what these people can do and what they can't do.

Schreibe auf, was die Personen können und was sie nicht können.

Example:

Charlie can swim but he can't ride a horse.

1. Gillian and Vanessa

2. David

3. Mrs Patel

4. Kenny

5. Karla

Now write what YOU can and can't do. The ideas in the box help you.

Schreibe auf, was DU kannst und was DU nicht kannst. Die Ideen im Kästchen helfen dir.

read a book • cook a meal • play hockey • ride a horse • sing • play the guitar

____

____

____

____

____

____

____

Lots of questions

David has a new pet and he has a lot of questions. Fill in the correct question word.

David hat ein neues Haustier und er hat viele Fragen. Trage die richtigen Fragewörter ein.

Tipp

Who heißt **wer** und **where** bedeutet **wo**!

who • where • when • what

1. ______________ can my new pet sleep? It can sleep in your room.
2. ______________ does my new pet eat? It eats bones and dog food.
3. ______________ can I take my new pet? You can take it to the park.
4. ______________ do I have to walk my pet? You have to walk it in the morning, in the afternoon and in the evening.
5. ______________ tricks can my pet do? Your pet can jump and roll over.

6. ______________ can help me with my pet? Your parents can help you with your pet.
7. ______________ do I take my pet to the vet[1] ? You take it to the vet when it is ill[2].
8. ______________ can I play with my pet? You can play with it in the park.

1 *vet* [vɛt]: Tierarzt 2 *ill* [ɪl]: krank

Pets and hobbies

Tipp

Schritt 1 – **Lies** erst alle Sätze.
Schritt 2 – **Verbinde** die Sätze zunächst ganz dünn mit Bleistift. Beginne mit den Sätzen, bei denen du dir ganz sicher bist.
Schritt 3 – **Prüfe**, ob alles passt.
Tipp: Vergiss nicht, die Nummern am Ende in die Tabelle einzutragen!

Read the following questions and match them with the correct short answer.

Lies die folgenden Fragen und verbinde sie mit den richtigen Kurzantworten.

A	Can you play the guitar?
B	Does your mother drive a blue car?
C	Are you twelve?
D	Have you got a pet?
E	Has your best friend got a bike?
F	Is your sister older than you?

1	Yes, he has.
2	No, I'm not.
3	No, I can't. I play the piano[1].
4	No, she doesn't.
5	Yes, she is.
6	Yes, I have.

A	
B	
C	
D	
E	
F	

Look at the information about Kenny and Ruby and write down five questions about them. Then answer your questions.

Lies die Informationen über Kenny und Ruby. Schreibe dann fünf Fragen über sie auf und beantworte sie.

	play		eat	feed
Ruby	in the living room	at 2 pm	oranges and apples	Rajiv
Kenny	in the park	at 5 pm	bones and dog food	father

Example: When does Ruby play?

1 *piano* [pɪ'ænəʊ]: Klavier

Look at the information about Kenny, Hoppity and Ruby and write down eight questions. Then answer your questions.

Lies die Informationen über Kenny, Hoppity und Ruby. Schreibe dann acht Fragen über sie auf und beantworte sie.

	play		eat	feed
Ruby	in the living room	at 2 pm	oranges and apples	Rajiv
Kenny	in the park	at 5 pm	bones and dog food	father
Hoppity	in the garden	at 11 am	carrots and spinach	Josh

Sentences and questions

Read the sentences and put in the correct preposition.

Lies die Sätze und setze die richtige Präposition ein.

about • for • on • to

1. Listen ________________ the CD.
2. The book club meets ________________ Mondays.
3. What do you need ________________ your sport?
4. Prepare a presentation ________________ your pet.
5. Turn the radio ________________ and listen to the song.
6. Write ________________ what you can or can't do!

Put these questions in the right order and answer them.

Bringe diese Fragen in die richtige Reihenfolge und beantworte sie.

1. ski • your grandfather • can ?

____

____

2. you • ride a bike • can ?

____

3. all your friends • can • play hockey?

____

____

4. drive a car • your parents • can ?

____

____

5. your teacher • write the numbers from 1 to 100 in English • can ?

____

____

Read the poster. Then write five questions about the club. The questions words in the box help you.

Lies das Poster. Schreibe dann fünf Fragen über den Club. Die Fragewörter im Kasten helfen dir.

Do you want to learn karate?
Anybody can join!

COME TO KARATE CLUB!

We have five free places at karate club. Every Wednesday afternoon, we train together at 2:30 pm. We meet in the gym at school. Bring comfortable clothes!

Sign up NOW!

when • how many • where • who • what

1. ______________________________
2. ______________________________
3. ______________________________
4. ______________________________
5. ______________________________

MEDIATION

At the market

Tipp

Gib in deinen eigenen Worten die **wichtigen Informationen** in der jeweils anderen Sprache wieder. Du musst **nicht Wort für Wort** übersetzen!

James and his German friend Ahmed are in a poster shop. Ahmed wants to buy a poster, but his English is not that good. James helps him. What does he say?
Use the phrases in the box.

James und sein deutscher Freund Ahmed sind in einem Postergeschäft. Ahmed möchte ein Poster kaufen, aber sein Englisch ist nicht so gut. James hilft ihm. Was sagt er?
Verwende die Sätze aus dem Kasten.

Tipp

Streiche die Sätze, die du bereits verwendet hast, in der Box **durch**. So behältst du leichter den Überblick.

I like it very much! How much is it? • Dankeschön und hier ist dein Wechselgeld – 50 Pence. • Can you show me the poster of Tower Bridge, please? • Moment – hier ist es. • Es kostet neun Pfund fünfzig.

Shop assistant: Hello, can I help you?

Ahmed: Ja, hallo. Können Sie mir bitte das Poster mit der Tower Bridge zeigen?

James: ______________________________

____

Shop assistant: Yes, just a minute. Here you are.

James: ______________________________

____

Ahmed: Es gefällt mir sehr gut! Was kostet es?

James: ______________________________

____

Shop assistant: This poster is nine pounds fifty.

James: ______________________________

____

Ahmed: *(hands the shopkeeper £10).*

Shop assistant: Thank you, and here is your change of fifty pence.

James: ____

____

Ahmed: Thank you very much and goodbye!

James and his German friend Ahmed are in a poster shop. Ahmed wants to buy a poster but his English is not that good. James helps him. What does he say?

James und sein deutscher Freund Ahmed sind in einem Postergeschäft. Ahmed möchte ein Poster kaufen, aber sein Englisch ist nicht so gut. James hilft ihm. Was sagt er?

Shop assistant: Hello, can I help you?

Ahmed: Ja, hallo. Können Sie mir bitte das Poster mit der Tower Bridge zeigen?

James: ____

____

____

____

____

Shop assistant: Yes, just a minute. Here you are.

James: ____

____

Ahmed: Es gefällt mir nicht so sehr. Kann ich bitte das andere Poster mit dem Buckingham Palace sehen?

James: ____

____

Shop assistant: Yes, of course!

James: ____

____

Ahmed: Das gefällt mir sehr gut. Was kostet es?

James: ____

____

Shop assistant: It's eight pounds seventy-five.

James: ______________________________

____

Ahmed: Das nehme ich. Kann ich das Poster mit dem Rennwagen[1] sehen?

James: ______________________________

____

____

Shop assistant: Sure!

James: ______________________________

____

Ahmed: Oh, das ist auch großartig! Was kostet das?

James: ______________________________

____

Shop assistant: It's five pounds.

James: ______________________________

____

Ahmed: Ich habe nur zwölf Pfund, aber ich würde gern beide[2] Poster kaufen.

James: ______________________________

____

Shop assistant: I can give you both posters for twelve pounds.

James: ______________________________

____

Ahmed: *(hands the shopkeeper 12 £)*

Shop assistant: Thank you and have a nice day.

James: ______________________________

____

Ahmed: Thank you very much and goodbye!

1 Rennwagen: *race car* [reɪs kaː] 2 beide: *both* [bəʊθ]

SPEAKING

School clubs (ab Ende Theme 3)

Look at the posters for these school clubs. There is some information missing. Ask your partner for the missing information and answer your partner's questions. The questions in the box (p. 67) help you.

Sieh dir die Poster für die Schul-AGs an. Es fehlen einige Informationen. Frage deinen Partner nach den Informationen und beantworte seine Fragen. Die Fragen in dem Kästchen (S. 67) helfen dir.

Look at the posters for these school clubs. There is some information missing. Ask your partner for the missing information and answer your partner's questions.

Sieh dir die Poster für die Schul-AGs an. Es fehlen einige Informationen. Frage deinen Partner nach den Informationen und beantworte seine Fragen.

Partner/-in A

________________ **Club**

Do you like ________________ ?

Everybody can come –
girls and boys!

When: 3 pm ________________

Where: sports field

With: ________________

Partner/-in B

Hockey Club

Do you like hockey?

Everybody can come –
boys and girls!

When: 3 pm, Monday

Where: sports field

With: Mr Morris

Partner/-in A

Drama Club

What: musical

When: 4 pm, Wednesday

Where: the school theatre

With: Mrs Johnson

Who: everybody – boys and girls
(must be 13 or older)

Partner/-in B

________________ Club

What: musical

When: 4 pm ________________

Where: ________________

With: Mrs Johnson

Who: ________________ –

________________ and ________________

(must be __________ or older)

☆ **Questions:**
What club is it?
What day is it?
Who is the teacher?

Questions:
What do we do?
What time does it start?
Where is the club?

Questions:
Who is welcome?
When does it start?
Where is it?

Questions:
What club is it?
What day is it?
Who is welcome?

☾ **Questions:**
What club … ?
What day … ?
Who is … ?

Questions:
What do … ?
What time … ?
Where is … ?

Questions:
Who is … ?
When does … ?
Where … ?

Questions:
What club … ?
What day … ?
Who is … ?

○ Rajiv and David (ab Ende Theme 3)

☆ ☾ **What can Rajiv and David do? What can't they do? Look at the list and say sentences.**

Was können Rajiv und David und was können sie nicht? Sieh dir die Tabelle an und sage dic Sätze.

	swim	ski	skate	hockey	football	☾ volleyball	gymnastic
Rajiv	✗	✓	✗	✓	✓	✗	✗
David	✓	✓	✓	✗	✓	✓	✗

Example: Rajiv can't swim but David can.

☼ **Now talk about yourself. What can and what can't you do?**

Sprich jetzt über dich selbst. Was kannst du und was nicht?

Example: I can swim but I can't play table tennis.

LISTENING

Tipp

Schritt 1 – **Vor dem ersten Hören:** Lies die Aufgabe(n).
Schritt 2 – **Beim ersten Hören:** Bearbeite die Aufgabe(n).
Schritt 3 – **Beim zweiten Hören:** Vervollständige und verbessere deine Antworten.

Nora's new room

Nora has got a new room. She tells her friend Anthony about it.

☆ **Listen to the phone call. What has Nora got in her new room? Tick ✓ the correct pictures.**

1. ☐ 

3. ☐ 

5. ☐ 

2. ☐ 

4. ☐ 

6. ☐ 

☆ ☾ **What else is in Nora's room? Tick ✓ the correct words.**

1. lamp	☐	5. computer	☐	9. poster	☐
2. bed	☐	6. cage	☐	10. teddy bear	☐
3. basketball	☐	7. shelf	☐	11. duvet	☐
4. couch	☐	8. pillow	☐		

Where does Nora put her things? Write down the numbers in the correct place.

1.

2.

3.

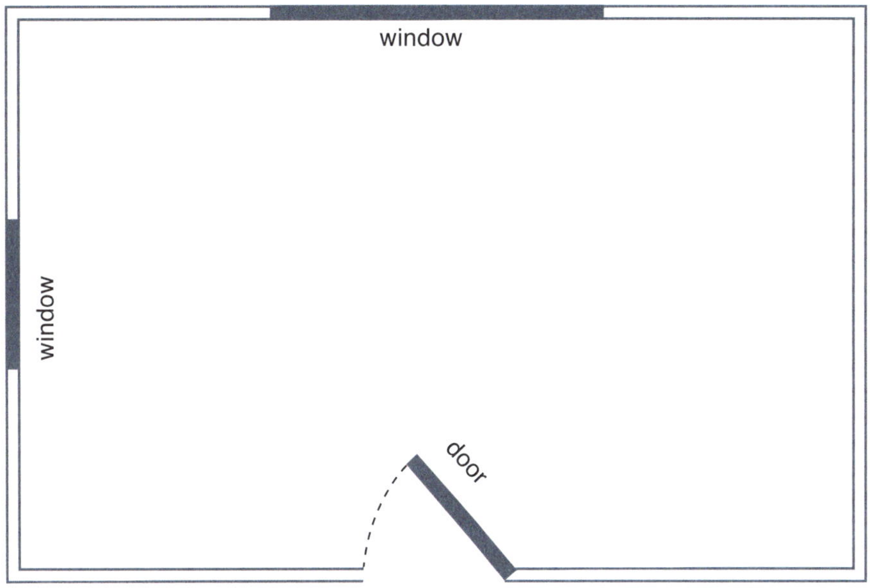

4.
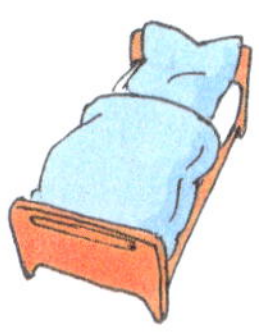

5.

6.

7.

Write short answers.

1. Where is Nora's bed?

under the big window

2. What colour is her chair?

3. Where is her teddy bear?

4. Where is her computer?

5. Where does Nora put her chocolate?

6. Why does she put it there?

7. When can Anthony come and see the room?

READING

Shopping for a sleepover

Tipp

Schritt 1 – **Vor dem Lesen:** Sieh dir die **Überschrift** an und überlege, worum es gehen könnte. Lies die Aufgabe(n) und überlege, was gesucht ist.

Schritt 2 – **Beim Lesen: Unterstreiche** die Informationen, die für die Aufgabe(n) gesucht werden.

Schritt 3 – **Beim zweiten Hören:** Vervollständige und verbessere deine Antworten.

Read the shopping dialogue.

Shopkeeper: Hello can I help you?
Josephine: Yes, please. I need some things for my sleepover tonight. I am sure Vanessa and Sheree are hungry when they come to my house!
Shopkeeper: What do you need?
Josephine: We want to make pizza. What kinds do you have?
Shopkeeper: I have sausage, bacon and extra cheese.
Josephine: Can I have two sausage and two extra cheese pizzas? How much are they?
Shopkeeper: Of course you can. The pizzas cost 99 pence each.
Josephine: We also want to make fruit salad.
Shopkeeper: I have bananas, apples, kiwis and strawberries[1].
Josephine: Can I have two bananas, two kiwis and some strawberries, please?
Shopkeeper: Sure! The fruit costs two pounds.
Josephine: Then we want to watch a film, so we need some crisps, drinks and chocolate.
Shopkeeper: We have apple juice, orange juice and water.
Josephine: I think we all like orange juice. Can I have two bottles, please?
Shopkeeper: No problem! One bottle costs 75 pence.
Josephine: Have you got dark chocolate?
Shopkeeper: Yes, I have.
Josephine: Can I have two bars[2] of chocolate, please?
Shopkeeper: Here you are. The chocolate costs one pound and 50 pence.
Josephine: Can I also have two bags of crisps, please?
Shopkeeper: Here you go. They cost two pounds. Is there anything else I can help you with?
Josephine: No, that's everything. Thank you!
Shopkeeper: OK, what have we got? Four pizzas, two bananas, two kiwis, some strawberries, two bottles of orange juice, two bars of dark chocolate, and two bags of crisps. That's ten pounds and 96 pence altogether, please.
Josephine: Here you are. *(Josephine gives the shopkeeper 20 pounds.)*
Shopkeeper: Thanks. Here is your change!
Josephine: Thank you! Goodbye!
Shopkeeper: Bye!

1 *strawberries* [strɔːbəriz]: Erdbeeren 2 *bar of chocolate* [baːr ɔv 'tʃɔkəlat]: Tafel Schokolade

Read the sentences. Tick ✓ wrong or right.

	right	wrong
1. Tonight is Josephine's birthday party.	☐	☐
2. Josephine and her friends want to make pizza.	☐	☐
3. Gillian and Karla can come to the party.	☐	☐
4. The fruit costs three pounds altogether.	☐	☐
5. In the evening the girls want to play games.	☐	☐
6. Josephine buys some dark chocolate.	☐	☐

Read the text again and correct the sentences.

1. Josephine buys five pizzas.

____

2. Josephine wants to make fruit salad with apples and bananas.

____

3. A bottle of orange juice costs 95 pence.

____

4. They want to eat something sweet with the movie.

____

5. The crisps cost one pound and 50 pence a bag.

____

6. Josephine pays 20 pounds altogether.

____

Read the text again and match the sentence halves.

A	Josephine wants to make	1	bacon and extra cheese pizzas.	A	
B	Josephine gives the shopkeeper	2	want to watch a film later.	B	
C	The shopkeeper has sausage,	3	and two bags of crisps.	C	
D	Josephine and her friends	4	fruit salad with bananas and kiwi and strawberries.	D	
E	Josephine buys two bars of chocolate	5	one pound fifty.	E	
F	Two bottles of orange juice cost	6	twenty pounds.	F	

Read the text again and answer the questions. Write complete sentences.

1. Who is coming to Josephine's sleepover?

2. What do the girls eat first?

3. How many pizzas does Josephine buy?

4. What kind of pizza does she choose?

5. What do they eat after the pizza?

6. How much does the fruit cost?

7. What kind of drinks does the shopkeeper offer?

8. How many bottles does Josephine buy?

9. How much does a bar of chocolate cost?

10. How much money does Josephine pay altogether?

11. How much change does Josephine get from the shopkeeper?

WRITING

Sharon's week

☆ **What does Sharon do every day? Look at the pictures and write about her week and say what she does on the different days. The phrases in the boxes help you. Write about 40 words.**

On Mondays … • On Tuesdays … • On Wednesdays … • On Thursdays … • On Fridays … • On Saturdays … • On Sundays …

visits her friend Sumaika (sometimes) • … does the cooking at home (never) • … stays in bed and reads a book (usually) • … watches TV (always) • … tidies her room (often) • … goes for a walk with her father (sometimes) • … plays tennis with her mother (often)

Example: On Mondays Sharon sometimes visits her friend Sumaika.

What does Sharon do every day? Look at the pictures (p. 73) and write about her week and say what she does on the different days. The phrases in the box help you. Write about 60 words.

… visit her friend Sumaika (sometimes) • … do the cooking at home (never) • … stay in bed and read a book (usually) • … watch TV (always) • … tidy her room (often) • … go for a walk with her father (sometimes) • … play tennis with her mother (often)

Example: On Mondays Sharon sometimes visits her friend Sumaika.

What does Sharon do every day? Look at the pictures (p. 73) and write about her week and say what she does on the different days. The phrases in the box help you. Write about 70 words.

On Mondays … • On Tuesdays … • On Wednesdays … • On Thursdays … • On Fridays … • On Saturdays … • On Sundays …

☼ **Now write about your own week. What do you do? Think about jobs at home and activitites.**

Mon	Tue	Wed	Thu	Fri	Sat	Sun
		1	2	3	4	5
6	7	8	9	10	11	12
13	14	15	16	17	18	19
20	21	22	23	24	25	26
27	28	29	30	31		

On Mondays I …

____

On Tuesdays I …

____

On Wednesdays I …

____

On Thursdays I …

____

On Fridays I …

____

On Saturdays I …

____

On Sundays I …

____

☼ **What is your favourite day of the week? Why?**

____

Who does what?

☆ Who does what in Sharon's family on Saturdays? Look at the list. Then write a text about Sharon and Josephine.

☾ ☼ Who does what in Sharon's family on Saturdays? Look at the list. Then write a text about Sharon's family.

	often vacuum the floors	always tidy his/her room	usually clean the kit-chen	never empty the dishwasher	sometimes take out the rubbish
Sharon	✓	✓			
Mr Batson					✓
Mrs Batson			✓		
Josephine		✓		✓	✓

On Saturdays Sharon often vacuums the floor.

☼ Now write about yourself and your family. What do you sometimes / never / usually do at home? Write about 50 words.

Example: My father sometimes washes the car.

WORDS AND GRAMMAR

What is in my room?

Label the picture. What is in this room? The words in the box help you.

shelf • cage • pillow • lamp • duvet • bed • TV • computer • wardrobe • chair • desk • posters

1. ______
2. ______
3. ______
4. ______
5. ______
6. ______
7. ______

8. ______
9. ______
10. ______
11. ______
12. ______

Label the picture. What is in this room? Name 12 things.

a) **Label the picture. What is in this room? Name 12 things.**

b) **Write where the things in the room are. Use the prepositions from the box.**

in • on • above • under • next to • behind

Example: The computer is on the desk.

Food and drink

☆ **Put the words into lists. Write the lists in alphabetical order.**

chocolate • cake • crisps • biscuits • apples • milk • orange juice • cheese • bananas • carrots • sausages • cookies • sandwiches • lemonade • water • beans

Tipp

Streiche die Begriffe, die du bereits verwendet hast, in der Box **durch**. So behältst du leichter den Überblick.

fruit	vegetables	drinks	sweet snacks	other

☾ **Put the words into lists and find a name for each list (there are some ideas in the orange box). Write the lists in alphabetical order.**

fruit • vegetables • drinks • sweet snacks • party food

chocolate • cake • crisps • biscuits • apples • tomatoes • milk • orange juice • cheese • bananas • carrots • sausages • sandwiches • lemonade • water • beans • ice cream • spinach

sweet snacks				

Write the words into lists and find a name for each list. Write the lists in alphabetical order.

chocolate • cake • crisps • biscuits • apples • tomatoes • milk • orange juice • cheese • bananas • carrots • sausages • sandwiches • lemonade • water • beans • ice cream • lemons • spinach

sweet snacks				party food

Jobs at home

Make phrases with the nouns or verbs from the box.

Tipp

Streiche die Begriffe, die du bereits verwendet hast, in der Box **durch**. So behältst du leichter den Überblick.

make • the rubbish • do • the cooking • vacuum • the bathroom • tidy • the pets

1. do ______________________
2. ______________________ the shopping
3. ______________________ my bed
4. clean ______________________
5. ______________________ the floor
6. feed ______________________
7. ______________________ my room
8. take out ______________________

Make phrases with the nouns or verbs from the box.

Tipp

Streiche die Begriffe, die du bereits verwendet hast, in der Box **durch**. So behältst du leichter den Überblick.

make • the rubbish • do • the cooking • vacuum • the bathroom • tidy • the pets • the children • empty

1. do ______
2. ______ the shopping
3. ______ my bed
4. clean ______
5. ______ the floor
6. feed ______
7. ______ my room
8. take out ______
9. look after ______
10. ______ the dishwasher

Make phrases with these nouns or verbs.

1. do ______
2. ______ the shopping
3. ______ my bed
4. clean ______
5. ______ the floor
6. feed ______
7. ______ my room
8. take out ______
9. look after ______
10. ______ the dishwasher

Find words from *Theme* 4.

1. Write down five jobs you or your parents do around the house.

______

______

______

2. Write down five things you need for a sleepover.

______

______

______

3. Write down the opposite of the following words.

tidy – ______________________

boring – ______________________

turn out – ______________________

in front of – ______________________

get out – ______________________

always – ______________________

evening – ______________________

dinner – ______________________

Pronouns and possessives

Complete the sentences. Use the words from the box.

> *words for a girl:* she, her • *words for a boy:* he, his •
> *words for two people or a group:* they, their •
> *words for you and your family, you and your friends, you and … :* we, our

1. Charlie lives in Hendon. ____________ has got three pets.

   ____________ pets are goldfish.

2. Vanessa and Gillian are friends. ____________ play football together.

   ____________ team has got ten players and a goalkeeper.

3. Josephine likes to play hockey. ____________ is in the hockey club at school.

   ____________ sister Sharon is also in the team.

4. My friends and I like to swim. ____________ go to the pool every day.

   ____________ swimming teacher is Mr Hacker.

5. At home my brother and I have jobs to do. ____________ clean the kitchen and tidy

   ____________ rooms.

6. Rajiv has got a pet. ____________ feeds ____________

   parrot every day and cleans the cage.

Complete the sentences. Use the words from the box.

she (2x) • her (2x) • he (2x) • his (2x) • they (2x) • their • we (2x) • our (2x)

Tipp

Setze in der Box **einen Haken** an jedes Pronomen, das du schon verwendet hast. So behältst du leichter den Überblick.

1. Charlie lives in Hendon. He has got three pets. ______ pets are goldfish.
2. Vanessa and Gillian are friends. ______ play football together. ______ team has got ten players and a goalkeeper.
3. Josephine likes to play hockey. ______ is in the hockey club at school. ______ sister Sharon is also in the team.
4. My friends and I like to swim. ______ go to the pool every day. ______ swimming teacher is Mr Hacker.
5. At home my brother and I have jobs to do. ______ clean the kitchen and tidy ______ rooms.
6. Rajiv has got a pet. ______ feeds ______ parrot every day and cleans the cage.

7. Mrs Marshall likes to go shopping. ______ buys fruit and vegetables for ______ family.
8. Mr Patel and his son have a hobby. ______ like fast cars.

Complete the sentences. Use the words from the box.

she • her • he • his • they • their • we • our

1. Charlie lives in Hendon. ______ has got three pets. ______ pets are goldfish.
2. Vanessa and Gillian are friends. ______ play football together. ______ team has got ten players and a goalkeeper.

3. Josephine likes to play hockey. ________________ is in the hockey club at school.

________________ sister Sharon is also in the team.

4. My friends and I like to swim. ________________ go to the pool all the time.

________________ swimming teacher is Mr Hacker.

5. At home me and my brother have jobs to do. ________________ clean the kitchen and tidy

________________ rooms.

6. Rajiv has got a pet. ________________ feeds ________________ parrot every day and cleans the cage.

7. Mrs Marshall likes to go shopping. ________________ buys fruit and vegetables for

________________ family.

8. Mr Patel and his son have a hobby. ________________ like fast cars.

9. David likes to eat sandwiches. ________________ makes ________________ lunch when he comes home from school.

10. My family and I go shopping every weekend. ________________ buy everything we need for the weekend. ________________ kitchen is a busy place.

Look at the sentences and fill in the correct pronouns and possessives.

Pronouns and possessives ...

... for a girl:

________________ – ________________

... for a boy:

________________ – ________________

... for two people or a group:

________________ – ________________

... for you and your family, you and your friends, you and ... :

________________ – ________________

What do the children do at home?

Write sentences with the words in brackets ( ).

Example: Tom never cleans his room.

1. Josh vacuums the floors. (always)
2. Gillian makes her bed. (sometimes)
3. Rajiv tidies his room. (often)
4. David does the washing up. (usually)
5. Vanessa cleans the kitchen. (never)
6. Charlie empties the dishwasher. (sometimes)

Unscramble the sentences and write them down.

1. vacuums • Josh • always • the floors
2. her bed • sometimes • makes • Gillian
3. Rajiv • his room • often • tidies
4. does • the washing up • David • usually
5. the kitchen • never • Vanessa • cleans
6. the dishwasher • empties • sometimes • Charlie

How often do the children do these jobs at home? Look at the table and write about the children.

job ↓	time →	often	usually	sometimes	never	always
vacuum the floors						Josh
make her bed				Gillian		
tidy his room		Rajiv				
do the washing up			David			
clean the kitchen					Vanessa	
empty the dishwasher				Charlie		
do the cooking			Josephine			

1. ______________________________

2. ______________________________

3. ______________________________

4. ______________________________

5. ______________________________

6. ______________________________

7. ______________________________

Who does it belong to?

Who do the animals and things belong to? Write down the sentences.

Example: This is Gillian's football.

1. Charlie ______________________________

2. Gillian ______________________________

3. Vanessa ____

4. Sharon ____

C Who do the animals and things belong to? Write down the sentences.

Example: This is Gillian's football.

1. Charlie ____

2. Gillian ____

3. Vanessa ____

4. Sharon ____

5. Mrs Marshall ____

6. Mr Patel ____

7. Rajiv ____

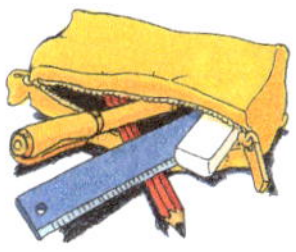

8. David ____

9. Ruby ____

10. Anna Coleman ____

Combine the two sentences into one sentence.

Examples:

Gillian has a football. It is black. Gillian's football is black.

Mrs Patel collects posters. They are big. Mrs Patel's posters are big.

1. Josh has got a rabbit. It is brown and white.

2. Karla plays with a basketball. It is new.

3. Mr Batson has got inline skates. They are new.

4. Dan likes football. His favourite team is Chelsea.

5. Anna Coleman plays tennis. Her new tennis partner is Mrs Batson.

6. David has got a new mobile phone. It is small.

7. Mahmut has got a new guitar. It is brown.

8. Vanessa tidies her room. It is untidy.

9. Eleanor drinks hot chocolate. It is sweet.

10. Sheree writes ghost stories. They are spooky.

11. Tom collects marbles. They are colourful.

12. Diego rides a horse. It is black and grey.

MEDIATION

Skyping with Grandma

Tipp

Gib in deinen eigenen Worten die **wichtigen Informationen** in der jeweils anderen Sprache wieder. Du musst **nicht Wort für Wort** übersetzen!

☆ **Tristan and his younger brother Tom talk to their grandmother in London on Skype. They tell her about the jobs they do around the house. Tom's English is not so good. Tristan helps him. What does Tristan say? The phrases in the box help you.**

Tipp

Streiche die Sätze, die du bereits verwendet hast, in der Box **durch**. So behältst du leichter den Überblick.

I sometimes make my bed. • Dad does the cooking every day. • Mum always cleans the bathroom. • I never tidy my room. • Tristan always takes out the rubbish.

Tom: Hello, Grandma, ich räume nie mein Zimmer auf!

Tristan: Hi Grandma, Tom says: " ____________________

Grandma: Tom, you can tidy your room.

Tristan: Grandma sagt, dass ____________________

Tom: Tristan bringt immer den Müll raus.

Tristan: Tom says: " ____________________

Grandma: Good, Tristan! That makes me very happy.

Tom: Papa kocht jeden Tag das Essen.

Tristan: ____________________

Tom: Und Mama putzt immer das Badezimmer.

Tristan: ____________________

Grandma: And what do you do, Tom?

Tristan: ____________________

Tom: Ich mache manchmal mein Bett.

Tristan: Tom says: " ____________________

Grandma: Well, that's a start.

Tristan and his younger brother Tom talk to their grandmother in London on Skype. They tell her about the jobs they do around the house. Tom's English is not so good. Tristan helps him. What does Tristan say?

Tom: Hello, Grandma, ich räume nie mein Zimmer auf!

Tristan: Hi Grandma, Tom says: ____________________

____

____

Grandma: Tom, you can tidy your room.

Tristan: Grandma sagt, dass ____________________

____

Tom: Tristan bringt immer den Müll raus.

Tristan: ____________________

Grandma: Good, Tristan! That makes me very happy.

Tom: Papa kocht jeden Tag das Essen.

Tristan: ____________________

____

Tom: Und Mama putzt immer das Badezimmer.

Tristan: ____________________

____

Grandma: And what do you do, Tom?

Tristan: ____________________

Tom: Ich mache manchmal mein Bett.

Tristan: Tom says: " ____________________

Grandma: Well, that's a start.

Tristan and his younger brother Tom talk to their grandmother in London on Skype. They tell her about the jobs they do around the house. Tom's English is not so good. Tristan helps him. What does Tristan say?

Tom: Hello, Grandma, ich räume nie mein Zimmer auf!

Tristan: Hi Grandma, Tom says: ______________________

____

____

Grandma: Tom, you can tidy your room.

Tristan: Grandma sagt, dass ______________________

____

Tom: Tristan bringt immer den Müll raus.

Tristan: ______________________

Grandma: Good, Tristan! That makes me very happy.

Tom: Papa kocht jeden Tag das Essen und wäscht immer das Geschirr ab.

Tristan: ______________________

____

Tom: Und Mama putzt immer das Badezimmer, saugt den Boden und putzt die Küche.

Tristan: ______________________

____

____

____

Grandma: And what do you do, Tom?

Tristan: ______________________

Tom: Ich mache manchmal mein Bett und ich helfe Papa beim Einkaufen.

Tristan: ______________________

____

____

Grandma: Well, that's a start.

SPEAKING

My room and your room

Tipp

Du musst das Bild für deinen/deine Partner/in **sehr genau** beschreiben. Achte auf alle **Details**!

Describe the picture on the next page to your partner. Then listen to your partner describe his/her picture. Draw the things in the empty room. Find the differences between your two pictures and tell your partner about them. The phrases in the box help you.

Example:
Partner/in A: There is a bed next to the window. There are posters …
Partner/in B: There is a lamp on the desk. The wardrobe is next to …

There is ... • There are ... • on the left ... • on the right ... • in the middle ... • in • on • under • next to • behind • above • shelves • desk • chair • wardrobe • lamp • posters • computer • books • cage • clothes

Describe the picture on the next page to your partner. Then listen to your partner describe his/her picture. Draw the things in the empty room. Find the differences between your two pictures and tell your partner about them. The phrases in the box help you.

Example:
Partner/in A: There is a bed next to the window. There are posters …
Partner/in B: There is a lamp on the desk. The wardrobe is next to …

There is ... • There are ... • in • on • under • next to • behind • above • shelves • desk • chair • wardrobe • lamp • posters • cage • clothes

Describe the picture on the next page to your partner. Then listen to your partner describe his/her picture. Draw the things in the empty room. Find the differences between your two pictures and tell your partner about them.

Partner A

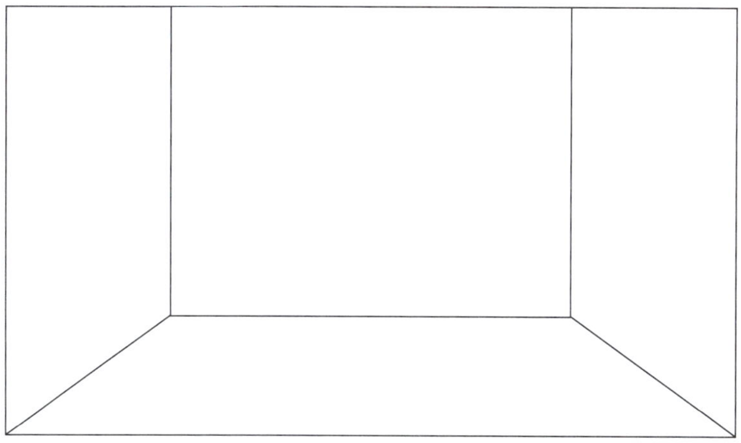

Partner B

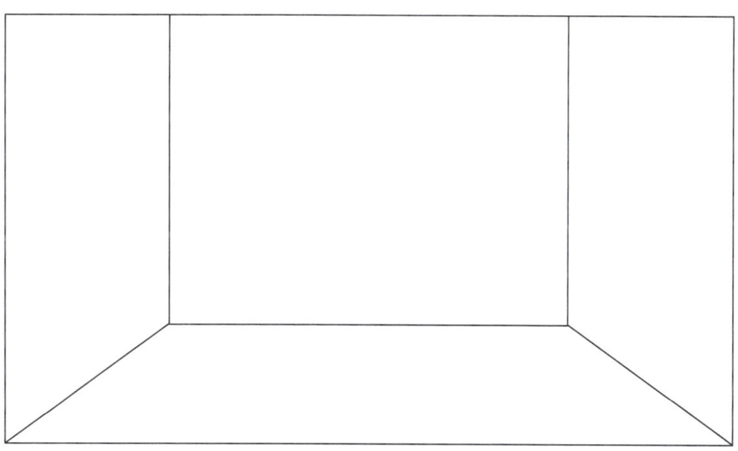

LISTENING

◯ Nadiya's favourite school day

Nadiya is talking to Daniel about her favourite school day.

Tipp

Schritt 1 – **Vor dem ersten Hören:** Lies die Aufgabe(n).
Schritt 2 – **Beim ersten Hören:** Bearbeite die Aufgabe(n).
Schritt 3 – **Beim zweiten Hören:** Vervollständige und verbessere deine Antworten.

Listen to the dialogue. Tick ✓ the correct information.

1. What day is Nadiya's favourite school day?

Nadiya's favourite schoolday is

- ☐ Monday
- ☐ Tuesday
- ☐ Thursday

2. What are Nadiya's favourite subjects?

Her favourite subjects are

☐ English	☐ German
☐ science	☐ history
☐ geography	☐ maths
☐ drama	☐ music

Which club does Nadiya go to?

A ☐ She plays hockey at 4:30 pm.
B ☐ She plays computer games in the computer club.
C ☐ She cooks her favourite meal in the cooking club.
D ☐ She visits the school library for the book club.

Listen to the dialogue again. What food and drink can you get in the canteen? What does Nadiya eat?

Food and drink in the canteen:

- ☐ sandwiches
- ☐ pizza
- ☐ fish and chips
- ☐ spaghetti
- ☐ apples
- ☐ salad
- ☐ milk
- ☐ water
- ☐ lemonade
- ☐ chocolate ice cream

Nadiya eats:

- ☐ sandwiches
- ☐ pizza
- ☐ fish and chips
- ☐ spaghetti
- ☐ apples
- ☐ salad
- ☐ milk
- ☐ water
- ☐ lemonade
- ☐ chocolate ice cream

Complete the sentences.

Tipp

Anders als im Deutschen gibt man im Englischen nicht die halbe Stunde **VOR** der vollen Stunde an, sondern die **NACH** der vollen Stunde. ‚Halb vier' heißt also *‚half past three'*. Bei Uhrzeiten wie z. B. 11:20 Uhr heißt es *‚eleven twenty'* oder *‚twenty minutes past eleven'*.

1. Usually school starts at ____________________
2. On Tuesdays, Nadiya goes to school ____________________
3. Nadiya's favourite teacher ____________________
4. She goes to school at ____________________
5. Daniel's second lesson is ____________________
6. Daniel likes music because they ____________________
7. Nadiya thinks geography in the afternoon is ____________________
8. Her favourite lesson is ____________________
9. At home Nadiya cooks her ____________________
10. School ends at ____________________

READING

Tipp

Schritt 1 – **Vor dem Lesen:** Sieh dir die **Überschrift** an und überlege, worum es gehen könnte. Lies die Aufgabe(n) und überlege, was gesucht ist.

Schritt 2 – **Beim Lesen: Unterstreiche** die Informationen, die für die Aufgabe(n) gesucht werden.

David's email

David writes an email to Luca, a pupil at his partner school in Germany.

Dear Luca,

My name is David Williams and I am eleven years old.
I'm at Hendon School. Let me tell you something about my family.

We live in a nice house in London. My mum's name is Alice. She is 37 years old. My dad's name is Thomas. He is 39. I haven't got any brothers or sisters. But I have got some cousins!

My father's parents are Janet and Ivor Williams. My grandmother is 65 and my grandfather is two years older[1]. They have four children: my dad, my uncle Morgan Williams – his wife is my aunt Fay Williams – my aunt Gwen Collins and my aunt Jane Swann. Gwen is divorced[2] from Paul. They have one child. Her name is Gillian. She is twelve. Gillian, her mum and her mum's girlfriend Anna live in Notting Hill. Gillian goes to Holland Park School. But in the afternoon, Gillian and I often play games together.

My aunt Jane Swann lives in Scotland with her husband Tom and their son Sam and their daughter Emma. Jane works in a school as a teacher. Her son Sam is twelve and Emma is fifteen years old. We don't meet very often. But when we do, Sam and I play football all the time. It's his favourite sport. His sister doesn't like any sports. She likes meeting her friends and reading books.

I have another grandmother. She's my mother's mother and her name is Louise Hamilton. Her husband, my grandfather, is called[3] James. They live in Brighton. My family and I always visit them in the summer holidays. They have got two daughters: my aunt Lisa Brown and my mum. Lisa's husband is Charles. They live in a house with Louise and James. Their son's name is Terry. He is fourteen years old. He is very good at skateboarding. But he also likes playing table tennis.

Please write soon and tell me about your family.

Bye,
David

1 *older* ['əʊldə]: älter 2 *is divorced from* [ɪz dɪ'vɔːst frɔm]: ist geschieden von 3 *is called* [ɪz kɔːld] wird genannt

Read David's email. Then complete the family tree with the numbers below. Write down the ages of the family members.

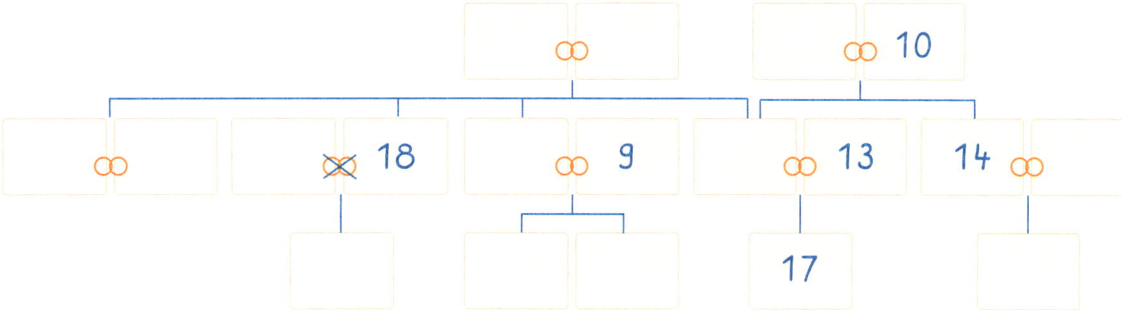

1 = Paul Collins

2 = Gillian Collins

3 = Janet Williams

4 = Jane Swann

5 = Sam Swann

6 = Ivor Williams

7 = Morgan Williams

8 = Louise Hamilton

9 = Tom Swann

10 = James Hamilton

11 = Fay Williams

12 = Terry Brown

13 = Alice Williams

14 = Lisa Brown

15 = Charles Brown

16 = Emma Swan

17 = David Williams

11 years old

18 = Gwen Collins

19 = Thomas Williams

Right or wrong? Read the sentences and tick ✓ the correct box.

	right	wrong
1. David has got a brother and a sister.	☐	☐
2. The Swanns live in Scotland.	☐	☐
3. Gillian goes to Hendon School.	☐	☐
4. Terry doesn't like table tennis.	☐	☐
5. Jane works in a hospital.	☐	☐
6. The Hamiltons live in London.	☐	☐
7. Charles is David's uncle.	☐	☐
8. The Williams family always go to Scotland in the summer holidays.	☐	☐
9. David and Gillian live in London.	☐	☐
10. Gwen has got two brothers.	☐	☐

Who is it? Write the names.

1. She doesn't like playing football.

2. Her parents are divorced.

3. They have one son and one daughter.

4. Her husband is 67 years old.

5. Her son is good at skateboarding.

6. His favourite sport is football.

7. He has got a sister who likes reading.

8. They always go to Brighton in the summer holidays.

9. She is fifteen years old.

10. Her husband is Charles.

11. She is Gwen's girlfriend.

12. She is David's mum.

WRITING

Tipp

Schritt 1 – **Vor dem Schreiben:** Prüfe, ob der Text eine bestimmte Form haben muss (z. B. E-Mail). Lege den Inhalt und die Reihenfolge fest.
Schritt 2 – **Schreibe** deinen Text.
Schritt 3 – **Überarbeite** deinen Text: Kontrolliere zuerst, ob alle Inhalte vorkommen. Prüfe dann, ob es grammatische Fehler gibt. Verbessere sie.

◯ Gillian's school day

This is what Gillian does on a school day.

A

B

C

D

E

F

A	
B	
C	
D	
E	
F	

☆ ☾ ☼ **Put the pictures in the correct order. Write numbers in the boxes.**

Write about Gillian's school day.

☆ **Choose four pictures. Write 40 words.**

☾ **Choose six pictures. Write 50–60 words.**

☼ **Choose six pictures and think of two more things Gillian does on a school day and write them about them too. Write about 70 words.**

Start like this: *Every school day Gillian gets up at 7 o'clock. Then she ...*

Your dream school day

☆ **Write about your dream school day. Answer the questions and write more sentences. Write 40 words.**

1. When does your dream school day start?
2. How do you get to school?
3. What subjects do you have?
4. When does your dream school day finish?

☾ **Write about your dream school day. Answer the questions and write more sentences. Write 50-60 words.**

1. When does your dream school day start?
2. How do you get to school?
3. What subjects do you have?
4. What do you eat for lunch?
5. What do you do in the breaks?
6. When does your dream school day finish?

☼ **Write about your dream school day. Answer the questions and write more sentences. Write 70 words.**

1. What does your dream school look like?
2. When does your dream school day start?
3. How do you get to school?
4. What subjects do you have?
5. What do you eat for lunch?
6. What do you do all day?
7. When does your dream school day finish?

WORDS AND GRAMMAR

Odd one out

Circle the odd one out.

1. Thursday • Monday • July • Tuesday
2. geography • maths • cake • art
3. by bus • by bike • by car • on foot
4. tie • registration • shirt • cap
5. torch • lesson • timetable • subject
6. break • balloon • assembly • registration
7. exercise • book • pencil • case • workbook • break
8. classroom • library • canteen • schoolbag

What is it?

Fill in the missing letters.

1. You can go there for lunch at school: ____ a ____ ____ ____ e ____
2. You put your school books in it: ____ ____ h ____ ____ ____ ____ a ____
3. British pupils wear it to school: u ____ ____ ____ o ____ ____
4. In British schools a school day starts and ends with:

   ____ e ____ ____ ____ t ____ ____ ____ ____ o ____
5. It's a subject in which you do sports: ____ ____
6. You can play with your friends in the ____ ____ ____ ____ k.
7. You learn to work with computers in ____ C ____.
8. In this subject you sing songs: ____ ____ ____ i ____

What is it?

Fill in the missing letters.

1. You can go there for lunch in school: ____ ____ ____ ____ ____ ____ ____
2. You put your school books in it: ____ ____ ____ ____ ____ ____ ____ ____ ____
3. British pupils wear it to school: ____ ____ ____ ____ ____ ____ ____

4. In British schools a school day starts and ends with:

___ ___ ___ ___ ___ ___ ___ ___ ___ ___ ___ ___

5. It's a subject in which you do sports: ___ ___

6. You can play with your friends in the ___ ___ ___ ___ ___

7. You learn to work with computers in ___ ___ ___

8. In this subject you sing songs: ___ ___ ___ ___ ___

Juliana's birthday calendar

This is Juliana's birthday calendar.

January	February	March	April	May	June
	3 rd Mum		15 th David	22 nd Adnan	
July	**August**	**September**	**October**	**November**	**December**
13 th me ☺	30 th Olivia		31 st Dad		

Write the names behind the correct dates. There are more dates than you need.

1. 03/02: ______
2. 30/08: Olivia
3. 13/07: ______
4. 15/04: ______
5. 31/10: ______
6. 22/05: ______

Write the birthdays in Juliana's calendar above.

1. 30/03: Abdul 2. 02/01: Carrie 3. 03/06: Fluffy the cat 4. 12/11: Jason

Whose birthday is it? Write the names.

1. the fifteenth day of the fourth month ______
2. the third day of the second month: ______
3. the last day of the tenth month: ______

4. the thirteenth day of the seventh month: ______

5. the thirtieth day of the eighth month: ______

6. the twenty-second day of the fifth month: ______

Write the dates.

1. the first day of the year: ______

2. the ninth day of the third month: ______

3. the twenty-third day of the sixth month: ______

Describe these days.

Example: 17 th April: the seventeenth day of the fourth month

1. 16 th January: ______

2. 29 th August: ______

3. 8 th July: ______

A birthday party

Tipp

Streiche die Silben, die du bereits verwendet hast, in der Box **durch**. So behältst du leichter den Überblick.

Find the words and write them down.

cand-	pic-	bal-	pre	calen-	dan-

-les	-nic	-loons	-sents	-dar	-cing

1. ______
2. ______
3. ______
4. ______
5. ______
6. ______

Match the verbs and the nouns.

Tipp

Schritt 1 – **Lies** erst alle Ausdrücke.
Schritt 2 – **Verbinde** die Ausdrücke zunächst ganz dünn mit Bleistift. Beginne mit den Sätzen, bei denen du dir ganz sicher bist.
Schritt 3 – **Prüfe**, ob alles passt.
Tipp: Vergiss nicht, die Nummern am Ende in die Tabelle einzutragen!

A	dance to
B	drink
C	eat
D	invite
E	make
F	play
G	pour

1	a muffin
2	friends
3	games
4	a pizza
5	tea
6	the drinks
7	music

A	
B	
C	
D	
E	
F	
G	

Add verbs to complete the phrases.

1. ____________ "Happy Birthday!"
2. ____________ a birthday card
3. ____________ magic tricks
4. ____________ presents
5. ____________ a picnic
6. ____________ a cake
7. ____________ out candles

What are they doing?

Look at the pictures. What are the people doing? What aren't they doing? Write six sentences. The words and phrases in the box help you.

feeding the cats • listening to the teacher • playing football • getting up • walking to school • having dinner

Example: He is talking to the teacher. He isn't doing his exercises.
They are watching TV. They aren't listening to the radio.

1. 

2. 

3. 

4. 

5. 

6. 

1. Erin ____________________

2. She ____________________

3. The pupils ____________________

4. Tom ____________________

5. The family ____________________

6. The boys ____________________

C Look at the pictures. What are the people doing? What aren't they doing? Write six sentences. The words and phrases in the box help you.

feed the cats • listen to the teacher • play football • get up • walk to school • have dinner

1. 

Erin ____________________

____

____

2. 

She ____________________

____

____

3. 

The pupils ____________________

____

____

4. 

Tom ____________________

____

____

5. 

The family ____________________

____

____

6. 

The boys ____________________

____

____

Look at the pictures. What are the people doing? What aren't they doing? Write nine sentences.

1. 

2. 

3. 

4. 

5. 

6. 

7. 

8. 

9. 

1. Erin ______________________________
2. She ______________________________
3. The pupils ______________________________
4. Tom ______________________________
5. The family ______________________________
6. The boys ______________________________
7. Janet ______________________________
8. Thomas ______________________________
9. David ______________________________

Gillian's school day

Complete the questions with words from the box.

Example: When **is** your birthday? Who **are** your friends?
When **do** you play football? Where **does** she live?

is • are • do • does

1. When ______________________ Gillian get up?
2. What ______________________ she want for breakfast?
3. Where ______________________ her schoolbag?
4. What ______________________ her favourite lessons?
5. How many pupils ______________________ in Gillian's class?
6. Who ______________________ her best friend at school?

7. How ______________________ she get to school?
8. When ______________________ her school day finish?
9. When ______________________ Gillian and her friends have lunch?
10. Why ______________________ Gillian hurry home?

Ask question about the underlined sentence parts.

Example: The birthday party finishes at 5 pm. → When does the birthday party finish?

1. Gillian is Rajiv's friend.

____

2. The friends meet at school every day.

____

3. School starts at 8:30 am.

____

4. Today I'm having a sandwich for lunch.

____

5. I get to school by bike every day.

____

MEDIATION

Tipp

Gib mit eigenen Worten die **wichtigen Informationen** in der jeweils **anderen Sprache** wieder. Du musst **nicht Wort für Wort** übersetzen!

Can you help out?

☆ **You and your cousin go shopping in Liverpool and want to buy some new clothes. But your cousin doesn't speak English well.**
Write down the correct sentences from the box.

How much is the T-shirt? • ... is looking for a green T-shirt. • Have you got this green T-shirt in small? • ... ob er uns helfen kann. • Die grünen T-Shirts sind da drüben. • Das kostet £ 10.50.

☾ **You and your cousin go shopping in Liverpool and want to buy some new clothes. But your cousin doesn't speak English well.**

Shop assistant: Hello, can I help you?

You: Er fragt, (1) ______________________________

Your cousin: Ich suche nach einem grünen T-Shirt.

You: My cousin (2) ______________________________

Shop assistant: The green T-shirts are over there.

You: (3) ______________________________

Your cousin: Toll! Dieses T-Shirt ist cool. Gibt es das auch in Größe S?

You: (4) ______________________________

Shop assistant: Yes, here you are.

You: Hier ist es.

Your cousin: Wieviel kostet das T-Shirt?

You: (5) ____________________

Shop assistant: It's ten pounds fifty.

You: (6) ____________________

You and your cousin go shopping in Liverpool and want to buy some new clothes. But your cousin doesn't speak English well.

Shop assistant: Hello, can I help you?

You: Er fragt, (1) ____________________

____

Your cousin: Ich suche nach einem grünen T-Shirt.

You: My cousin (2) ____________________

Shop assistant: The green T-shirts are over there.

You: (3) ____________________

Your cousin: Toll! Dieses T-Shirt ist cool. Gibt es das auch in Größe S?

You: (4) ____________________

Shop assistant: Yes, here you are.

You: Hier ist es.

Your cousin: Wieviel kostet das T-Shirt?

You: (5) ____________________

Shop assistant: It's ten pounds fifty.

You: (6) ____________________

Your cousin: Hier sind £15.

You: (7) ____________________

Shop assistant: And here's £4.50 back.

You: (8) ____________________

SPEAKING

On the way to school

Tipp

Bei dieser Aufgabe musst du den Stundenplan durch **gezielte Fragen** an deinen Partner beantworten. Sprich in **ganzen Sätzen**.
Beachte bei den Zeitangaben, dass *‚am‘* für Uhrzeiten von 0 Uhr bis 12 Uhr steht und dass *‚pm‘* für Uhrzeiten von 12 Uhr bis 24 Uhr steht.

Talk to your partner about your timetable and ask for the missing information. The phrases in the box help you.

When does … start/end? • What is the first/second/ … lesson on … ? • How long … ?

Partner/in A

time/day	Monday	Tuesday	Wednesday	Thursday	Friday
08:00 – ______	history	English	science	maths	PE
break					
09:45 – 11:05	English	geography	______	German	music
break					
______ – 12:50	______	maths	art	ICT	drama
lunch					
01:50 – 03:10	–	______	–	–	–

Partner/in B

time/day	Monday	Tuesday	Wednesday	Thursday	Friday
08:00 – 09:20	history	______	science	maths	PE
break					
______ – 11:05	English	geography	RE	German	______
break					
11:30 – 12:50	German	maths	art	______	drama
lunch					
01:50 – ______	–	PE	–	–	–

Talk to your partner about your timetable and ask for the missing information. The phrases in the box help you.

When does … start/end? • What is the first/second/ … lesson on … ? • How long … ?

Partner/in A

time/day	Monday	Tuesday	Wednesday	Thursday	Friday
08:00 – ____	history	English	science	____	PE
break					
____ – 11:05	English	____	____	German	music
break					
11:30 – ____	____	maths	art	ICT	____
lunch					
____ – 03:10	–	____	–	–	–

Partner/in B

time/day	Monday	Tuesday	Wednesday	Thursday	Friday
____ – 09:20	history	____	____	maths	PE
break					
09:45 – ____	____	geography	RE	German	____
break					
____ – 12:50	German	____	art	____	drama
lunch					
01:50 – ____	–	PE	–	–	–

☼ Talk to your partner about your timetable and ask for the missing information. What else can you say about the timetable? (e.g. How many lessons do the students have?

Partner/in A

Time/day	Monday	Tuesday	Wednesday	Thursday	Friday
08:00 – ______	history	English	science	______	PE
break					
______ – 11:05	English	______	______	German	music
break					
11:30 – ______	______	maths	art	ICT	______
lunch					
______ – 03:10	–	______	–	–	–

Partner/in B

Time/day	Monday	Tuesday	Wednesday	Thursday	Friday
______ – 09:20	history	______	______	maths	PE
break					
09:45 – ______	______	geography	RE	German	______
break					
______ – 12:50	German	______	art	______	drama
lunch					
01:50 – ______	–	PE	–	–	–

LISTENING

Tipp

Schritt 1 – **Vor dem ersten Hören:** Lies die Aufgabe(n).
Schritt 2 – **Beim ersten Hören:** Bearbeite die Aufgabe(n).
Schritt 3 – **Beim zweiten Hören:** Vervollständige und verbessere deine Antworten.

A family weekend at the farm

The Buchanans went to a farm for a weekend. Now Allyson tells William everything about her family's trip.

☆ **Listen to the conversation. What kind of animals did they like? Match the people and the animals. Draw lines. There are more pictures than you need.**

Mum Dad Allyson Josephine Liam

☆ ☾ **Listen again. Then write short answers.**

1. Where is the farm?

____

2. What did Allyson do?

____

3. When did they go home?

____

Read the sentences. Then listen to the conversation and tick ✓ the correct answer.

1. The Buchanans went to
   - A ☐ the beach.
   - B ☐ a farm.
   - C ☐ London.

2. The Buchanans family went to the farm by car because
   - A ☐ the train tickets cost too much.
   - B ☐ there was no bus to the farm.
   - C ☐ they wanted to go to London before they went to the farm.

3. Allyson's favourite animals were
   - A ☐ the ducks.
   - B ☐ the ponies
   - C ☐ the horses.

4. The horse was perfect for Allyson because
   - A ☐ it was very small.
   - B ☐ Allyson liked the horse's name.
   - C ☐ it was not too big.

5. Liam was excited because
   - A ☐ he rode on the tractor with the farmer.
   - B ☐ he rode a bull.
   - C ☐ they had a family picnic.

6. The Buchanans left the farm at
   - A ☐ 10:30 am.
   - B ☐ 11:30 am.
   - C ☐ 12:30 am.

Listen again. Answer the questions in complete sentences.

1. Where did Mr and Mrs Buchanan want to go?

____

____

____

2. What did the Buchanans do on Friday evening?

____

____

3. What happened to the boy who ran away from the bull?

____

____

4. Why didn't the family have much time on Sunday?

____

____

READING

Tipp

Schritt 1 – **Vor dem Lesen:** Sieh dir die **Überschrift** an und überlege, worum es gehen könnte. Lies die Aufgabe(n) und überlege, was gesucht ist.
Schritt 2 – **Beim Lesen: Unterstreiche** die Informationen, die für die Aufgabe(n) gesucht werden.

Holidays at the summer camp

☆ **Read about Paul's time at the summer camp. What activities did Paul do at the summer camp? Tick ✓ the correct pictures (p. 115 – p. 116). There are more pictures than you need.**

Dear Aisha,

How are you? I'm fine. I'm writing to you from the summer camp in Scotland. It's the end of July and the camp is almost over. But I want to tell you about some of the things I did here in the last three weeks.
In the first week the weather was not very good. That's why we did a lot things inside. We could play card games, do a computer course or learn how to draw animals. But I took some guitar lessons. Now can I can play the guitar.
On Sunday my parents visited me at the camp. They stayed till the evening and we had dinner at the camp centre. The food was really nice and we had a good time together. When Mum and Dad went home, I was a little sad. But my new friend Tom made me laugh again. We played football in the evening.
The weather was good in the second and third week of the camp. So we did a lot of sport outside. There was a inline skating and skateboarding course. I was in the basketball team. Our team was very good. We won a match against the other team and got a prize: a basketball for the team. That was really cool!
I did a lot of swimming, too. I wasn't so good at swimming before I came to the camp. But I got better each day. In the end I was second in the swimming race.
In the third week we could choose between going to a zoo and going to a farm. I went to the farm. We worked with the farmer. We fed the animals and rode on the tractor across the fields. That was a lot of fun!
Next Wednesday I'm home again. Maybe we can meet. Then I can show you all the pictures on my camera. And I can show you how to play the guitar.

See you soon
Paul

1. ☐ 

2. ☐ 

3. ☐ 

4. ☐ 

5. ☐ 

6. ☐ 

7. ☐ 

8. ☐ 

9. ☐ 

Read about Paul's time at the summer camp.

Dear Aisha,

How are you? I'm fine. I'm writing to you from the summer camp in Scotland. It's the end of July and the camp is almost over. But I want to tell you about some of the things I did here in the last three weeks.

In the first week the weather was not very good. That's why we did a lot things inside. We could play card games, do a computer course or learn how to draw animals. But I took some guitar lessons. Now can I can play the guitar. Maybe we can sing some songs together and I can play the guitar.

On Sunday my parents visited me at the camp. They stayed till the evening and we had dinner at the camp centre. The food was really nice and we had a good time together. When Mum and Dad went home, I was a little sad. But my new friend Tom made me laugh again. We played football in the evening.

The weather was good in the second and third week of the camp. So we did a lot of sport outside. There was a skating and skateboarding course and dancing lessons for the girls. But I don't like skateboarding and skating. So I was in the basketball team. Our team was really good. We won a match against the other team and got a prize: a basketball for the team. That was really cool!

I did a lot of swimming, too. I wasn't so good at swimming before I came to the camp. But I got better each day. In the end I was second in the swimming race.

In the third week we could choose between going to a zoo and going to a farm. At the zoo there were a lot of wild animals. And there was a big playground. The children who went there told me everything about it. I went to the farm. We worked with the farmer. We fed the animals and rode the tractor across the fields. That was a lot of fun.

Next Wednesday I'm home again. Maybe we can meet. Then I can show you all the pictures on my camera. And I can show you how to play the guitar.

See you soon,
Paul

What happened at the summer camp? Match the sentences.

A	The summer camp	1	bad in week one.		A	
B	The weather was	2	home on Wednesday.		B	
C	Paul learned	3	learn to do skating and skateboarding.		C	
D	Paul's parents came to the camp	4	at the first weekend.		D	
E	In weeks two and three Paul did a lot of sport	5	because the weather was good.		E	
F	Paul's basketball team	6	swimming every day.		F	
G	At the camp you could	7	to play the guitar.		G	
H	Paul went	8	to work on the farm.		H	
I	Paul wanted	9	was in Scotland.		I	
J	He goes	10	won a basketball.		J	

What happened at the summer camp? Tick ✓ the correct box.

1. The summer camp was in
A ☐ England.
B ☐ Scotland.
C ☐ Ireland.

2. Paul went there for
A ☐ the summer holidays.
B ☐ three weeks.
C ☐ three days.

3. He learned how to
A ☐ work with a computer.
B ☐ play the guitar.
C ☐ draw animals.

4. Paul's parents
A ☐ were sad when they went home.
B ☐ came to the camp on Saturday.
C ☐ had dinner with Paul at the camp centre.

5. In week two Paul
A ☐ and his team played basketball.
B ☐ learned how to skate.
C ☐ won a football match.

6. His team
A ☐ was very good at swimming before the camp.
B ☐ took some dancing lessons.
C ☐ won a basketball.

7. In the third week Paul
A ☐ worked on a farm.
B ☐ went to the playground in the zoo.
C ☐ played football with Tom.

8. When Paul is home again
A ☐ he wants to meet Aisha.
B ☐ he wants to go to the photo club at school.
C ☐ he wants to play the guitar in a band.

WRITING

Tipp

Schritt 1 – **Vor dem Schreiben:** Prüfe, ob der Text eine bestimmte Form haben muss (z. B. E-Mail). Lege den Inhalt und die Reihenfolge fest.
Schritt 2 – **Schreibe** deinen Text.
Schritt 3 – **Überarbeite** deinen Text: Kontrolliere zuerst, ob alle Inhalte vorkommen. Prüfe dann, ob es grammatische Fehler gibt. Verbessere sie.

Things to do on a farm

1.

2.

3.

4.

☆ **Look at the pictures. Then write down what you want to do and what you don't want to do on a farm. Write about 50 words. The words in the box help you.**

I like/don't like … • I want to/don't want to … because… • You can/can't …
It's fun/interesting/boring/ … • I'd like to …

☾ **Look at the pictures. Then write down what you want to do and what you don't want to do on a farm. Write about 60 words.**

☼ **Look at the pictures. Then write down what you want to do and what you don't want to do on a farm. Write about 70 words. You can use your own ideas.**

My last summer holidays

☆ **Write about what you did in your last summer holidays. Write about 50 words. The words in the box help you.**

visited • was/were • went to • played • liked • did • went swimming/shopping/ …

☾ **Write about what you did in your last summer holidays. Write about 60 words.**

☼ **Write about what you did in your last summer holidays. Write about 70 words.**

In the last summer holidays

WORDS AND GRAMMAR

Words, words, words

☆ **Complete the words. Then add one word to each list.**

animals	places	people
s _ _ _ p	f _ r _	b _ k _ _
_ u _ l	_ i _ _ d	b _ _ i _ n _ r
_ o _	c _ _ t l _	_ a _ _ _ r

☾ **Complete the words. Then add two words to each list.**

actions (= what you do)	places	people
l _ _ g _	f _ r _	b _ k _ _
_ ru _ h	_ i _ _ d	p _ _ f _ ss _ _ _ al
_ r _ _ s	_ _ f _ r _ _ i _ _ s _ _ n _	k _ _ _ r

☼ **Complete the words. Then add four words to each list.**

nouns	verbs	adjectives
h _ l _ _ _ y	m _ v _	r _ i _ y
b _ i _ d _	s _ o _ t	h _ _ h
_ r _ _ t _ r	_ a _ d	_ xc _ t _ d
m _ _ t _	w _ v _	s _ _ p _ i _ _ d

Opposites

Tipp

Streiche die Begriffe, die du bereits verwendet hast, in der Box **durch**. So behältst du leichter den Überblick.

☆ **Match the opposites and write them down.**

out	summer
cold	hot
late	up
winter	early
down	true
false	in

☾ **Match the opposites and write them down.**

out	summer
beginner	true
cold	early
exciting	up
late	tomorrow
rainy	hot
winter	in
down	sunny
false	boring
indoor	outdoor
on the left	on the right
yesterday	professional

Match the opposites and write them down. Add two opposites to the list.

out	tomorrow
cold	in
late	hot
winter	early
down	up
false	far
indoor	on the right
on the left	true
yesterday	summer
near	outdoor

______________________ ______________________

______________________ ______________________

______________________ ______________________

______________________ ______________________

______________________ ______________________

______________________ ______________________

Phrases

Tipp

Streiche die Begriffe, die du bereits verwendet hast, in der Box **durch**. So behältst du leichter den Überblick.

Match the words from the box with the verbs.

well • on holiday • at/to somebody • a good time • something up • a picnic • the pigs • a crush on somebody

1. feed ______________________
2. have ______________________
3. pick ______________________
4. have ______________________
5. get on ______________________
6. have ______________________
7. be ______________________
8. wave ______________________

Match the phrases from the box with the verbs. There are more phrases than you need.

a plane • well • on holiday • at/to somebody • a good time • spaghetti • a film • something up • a picnic • the pigs • a lot of fun • on a tractor • to the swimming pool • a door • someone home

1. feed ______________
2. have ______________
3. pick ______________
4. have ______________
5. get on ______________
6. have ______________
7. be ______________
8. wave ______________
9. ride ______________
10. eat ______________
11. go ______________
12. open ______________

What can you do on a trip to a farm? Add the verbs.

1. ______________ the chicken
2. ______________ on tractor
3. ______________ in the fields
4. ______________ to the hen house
5. ______________ a picnic
6. ______________ the farmer
7. ______________ a bridge
8. ______________ in the pond
9. ______________ the animals
10. ______________ photos

Gillian's weekend

Fill in the simple past forms of the verbs in brackets.

Example: Yesterday Gillian ___played___ (play) football. She ___came___ (come) home late.

Last weekend Gillian and her family ______________ (go) to a farm in Wales.

There ______________ (be) ducks, chicken, sheep, goats, cows and a bull on the farm. In the afternoon Gillian and her family ______________ (help) the farmer.

Gillian ______________ (work) with the farmer in the field.

After the work was finished, Gillian ______________ (ride) a pony. At 6 o'clock in the evening the farmer ______________ (invite) the Collins family to have dinner with him. What an interesting day!

Fill in the simple past forms of the verbs in the box.

Example: Yesterday Gillian ___played___ football. She ___came___ home late.

be • feed • go • have • help • invite • love • ride • work

Last weekend Gillian and her family ____________ to a farm in Wales. There ____________ ducks, chicken, sheep, goats, cows and a bull on the farm. At 1 pm the Collinses ____________ a picnic in the picnic area. In the afternoon Gillian ____________ the farmer. Anna Coleman and Mrs Collins ____________ all the animals. Gillian ____________ with the farmer in the fields. After the work was finished, Gillian ____________ a pony. She really ____________ that. At 6 o'clock in the evening the farmer ____________ the Collinses to have dinner with him. What an interesting day!

Fill in the simple past forms of the verbs in the box.

arrive • be • feed • go • have • help • invite • love • work • ride • show • start

Last weekend Gillian and her family ____________ to a farm in Wales. They ____________ at 10 am in Notting Hill. After two hours they ____________ at the farm. The farmer ____________ them all the animals. There ____________ ducks, chicken, sheep, goats, cows and a bull. At 1 pm the Collinses ____________ a picnic in the picnic area. In the afternoon Gillian ____________ the farmer. Anna Coleman and Mrs Collins ____________ the animals. Gillian ____________ with the farmer in the fields. After the work was finished, Gillian ____________ a pony. She really ____________ that. At 6 o'clock in the evening the farmer ____________ the Collinses to have dinner with him. What an interesting day!

What did you do last week?

☆ **Write four sentences about what you did last week. The ideas in the box help you.**

Example: On Monday I ___played___ football.

go to school • read a book • watch TV • visit friends

☾ **Write four sentences about what you did last week.**

Example: On Monday I ___played___ football.

☼ **Write six sentences about what you did last week.**

Just a normal day

☆ **It's just a normal day. Look at the pictures. What are the people doing? Choose <u>four</u> pictures. Write about the people's activities. The verbs in the box help you. Use *–ing* forms.**

☾ **It's just a normal day. Look at the pictures. What are the people doing? Write about the people's activities. The verbs in the box help you. Use *–ing* forms.**

Examples: is eating, are walking

brush her teeth • play tennis • trys to read a book • play computer games • sleep • ride on a tractor

1.  Rajiv and Gillian

2.  The boy

3.  David and Charlie

4.  Sally

5.  Lisa

6.  David

☼ **It's just a normal day. Look at the pictures. What are the people doing? Write about the people's activities. Use *–ing* forms.**

MEDIATION

Tipp

Gib mit eigenen Worten die **wichtigen Informationen** in der jeweils **anderen Sprache** wieder. Du musst **nicht Wort für Wort** übersetzen!

At the holiday camp

You and your German friend Niclas are going to a holiday camp in your summer holidays. You have got a flyer with all the activities you can do at the summer camp.

Things you can do and learn at our holiday camp:

1 Do you want to play the guitar?

There is a guitar course every Tuesday and Thursday at 3 pm.

Camp cafeteria

2 Games, games, games

If you like playing card and board games, there is a game evening every Monday.

Room 12, 7 pm
You can bring your favourite games!

3 Do you want to be a famous basketball player?

Come to our basketball training. There is a match at the end of the camp and you can win a cool prize!

Playing field
Mondays, 10 am

4 Photography course

Learn how to take good pictures in our photography course.

Every Sunday morning, 9.30 am,
Main hall

Bring your camera!

5 Cakes and biscuits competition

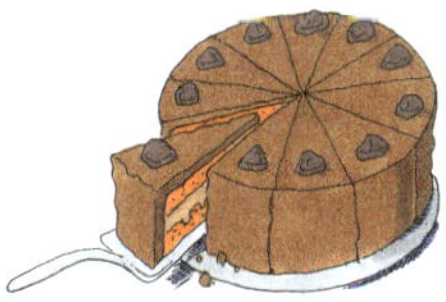

Make your favourite cakes and biscuits. The best cakes and biscuits win a prize – a cookbook!

First Saturday at the camp, 3 pm, Camp kitchen

Write an email to Niclas about <u>two</u> activities and tell him

- what you can do.
- where you can do these activities.
- at what time they start.
- what is important for these activities.

Tipp

Denke daran, dass du deinem Freund auf **Deutsch** schreibst. Beachte bei den Zeitangaben, dass im Englischen *‚am'* für Uhrzeiten von 0 bis 12 Uhr steht und dass *‚pm'* für Uhrzeiten von 12 bis 24 Uhr steht.

Write an email to Niclas about <u>four</u> activities and tell him

- what you can do.
- where you can do these activities.
- at what time they start.
- what is important for these activities.

Write an email to Niclas about <u>all</u> the activities and tell him

- what you can do.
- where you can do these activities.
- at what time they start.
- what is important for these activities.

SPEAKING

At the funny farm

Tipp

Wenn du ein Bild auf Englisch beschreiben sollst, sage so viel wie möglich über den **Inhalt** des Bildes.

Schritt 1 – Überlege, welche Wörter du zum Bild kennst.
Schritt 2 – Sprich in **ganzen Sätzen**.
Schritt 3 – Zum Üben kannst du sie hier unter dem Bild notieren.
Achtung: In der Prüfung musst du sie dir merken!

Words and phrases:

____

____

____

____

____

Describe the picture of this funny farm. Talk about the animals and what they are doing. The phrases in the box help you.

I can see … • There is/There are …

Describe the picture of this funny farm. Talk about the animals and what they are doing.

Describe the picture of this funny farm. Talk about the animals and what they are doing. Talk about what you would do at a farm.

Making plans for the weekend

Partner/-in A

Du rufst deinen Freund/deine Freundin an und möchtest mit ihm/ihr das gemeinsame Wochenende auf dem Bauernhof planen.

1 Begrüße deinen Freund/deine Freundin.

3 Sage, dass es dir gut geht und dass du dich auf das Wochenende auf dem Bauernhof freust.

5 Antworte, dass du deinen Freund/deine Freundin um 15 Uhr abholst. Frage, was ihr auf der Farm machen wollt.

7 Sage, dass dir die Ideen gefallen, und schlage vor, dass ihr auch noch Traktor fahren könnt.

9 Schlage zwei Aktivitäten vor, die ihr machen könnt, falls das Wetter am Wochenende schlecht ist.

11 Sage, dass du nun zu Abend essen musst und verabschiede dich.

Hello!
I'm …
I'm looking forward to …

Partner/-in B

Dein Freund/Deine Freundin ruft dich an, um das gemeinsame Wochenende auf dem Bauernhof zu planen.

2 Freue dich über den Anruf deines Freundes/deiner Freundin und frage wie es ihm/ihr geht.

4 Antworte, dass du dich auch freust und frage, wann ihr zum Bauernhof fahren wollt.

6 Schlage folgende Dinge vor: Tiere füttern, Picknick machen, reiten

8 Sage, dass das gut klingt.

10 Mache zwei weitere Vorschläge.

12 Verabschiede dich ebenso.

Hi! Great to hear from … !
How …?
I'm looking forward to …, too.
When are we going to the farm?

Lösungen

THEME 1: People and places

S. 6 Listening: Meet Greg and Mathilda

a) 1. Miller
2. eight
3. a sister
4. football

b) brother and sister, skateboard, tennis, guitar, pizza

S. 7 Listening: Meet Balraj and Fiona

a)
1. Balraj, Fiona
2. Balraj
3. Fiona
4. Balraj, Fiona
5. Balraj
6. Fiona
7. Fiona
8. Balraj, Fiona

b) name: Balraj
age: twelve years
brothers or sisters: one sister, eight years old
town: London
hobbies: basketball, music

name: Fiona
age: twelve years
brothers or sisters: no brothers or sisters
town: London
hobbies: football, music

S. 8 Reading: Kenny's blog

a)
1. wrong
2. right
3. right
4. wrong
5. wrong
6. right

b) name: Kenny Hoover
age: three years
town: Hendon/London
best friend: Skipper
family: David Williams and his parents
favourite hobby: play with a ball

S. 9 Writing: This is me

individuelle Schülerlösung, Beispiel:
a) name: Sophia Mau
town: Frankfurt
age: 11
family: Susanne & Christoph, sister Eva
hobby: go swimming
best friend: Ceren
favourite food: pizza

b) My name is Sophia Mau. I am from Frankfurt and I am eleven years old. My parents are Susanne and Christoph and I have got a sister. I like to go swimming in my free time. My best friend is Ceren. My favourite food is pizza.

S. 10 Writing: Hi, I'm Rajiv

Lösungsvorschlag:
Hi, my name is Rajiv Patel and I am twelve years old. I live in Notting Hill in London with my parents and my sister Sheree. My parents are from India. I can speak English and Hindi. My hobbies are cooking and playing the guitar. I also have got a parrot, Ruby. My best friends are Gillian and Karla.

S. 11 Writing: Welcome to Notting Hill

a) *Lösungsvorschlag*:
<u>sights</u>: market in Portobello Road (every Saturday), Holland Park, famous street Notting Hill Gate
<u>activities</u>: shopping, playing in the park
<u>places</u>: cinema, playground, shops, market in London
<u>how to get there</u>: by bus, by tube

b) *Lösungsvorschlag*:
Notting Hill is an area in London. There is a famous street, Notting Hill Gate. Many people go there by bus or by tube. There are many shops and there is a market in Portobello Road every Saturday. There is also a park, Holland Park. You can go to the playground or the café or see the flowers.

S. 12 Words and Grammar: Pets

rabbit cat goldfish dog parrot mouse

S. 12 Words and Grammar: Weather Words

1. In April there is a lot of <u>rain</u>.
2. In summer it is very <u>hot</u>.
3. The <u>sun</u> shines a lot in July.
4. You can fly a kite when it is <u>windy</u>.
5. May is in <u>spring</u>.
6. In winter we can build a <u>snowman</u>.

S. 13 Words and Grammar: People and Places

1. parents
2. cousin
3. friend
4. neighbour
5. Tuesday

S. 13 Words and Grammar: Pets and food

a) pets: parrot, pig, rabbit, hamster
food: tomato, ice cream, banana, cheese

b) *Lösungsbeispiele*:
pets: dog, pig, goldfish, mouse
food: apple, orange, pizza, hamburger

c) places in town: market, park, playground, swimming pool

S. 14–15 Words and Grammar: Phrases

a) A4 B6 C1 D3 E2 F5

b)
1. listen to music
2. talk to your partner
3. play tennis
4. speak English
5. look at the picture
6. go to the swimming pool
7. wear a T-Shirt
8. sit on a couch

c) *Lösungsvorschlag*:
1. play football
2. make your own chant
3. have a pet
4. be in a room
5. tell a story
6. like ice cream
7. ride a bike
8. swim in the pool

S. 15 Words and Grammar: Gillian and David

1. is
2. are
3. is
4. isn't
5. is
6. is
7. am
8. isn't
9. am
10. am not / am
11. is

S. 16–17 Words and Grammar: Rajiv and Karla

a)

	long form		short form	
	+	–	+	–
I	am	am not	'm	'm not
you	are	are not	're	aren't
he/she/ it	is	is not	's	isn't
we	are	are not	're	aren't
you	are	are not	're	aren't
they	are	are not	're	aren't

b)
1. Rajiv is twelve.
2. His parents are from India.
3. I am from Notting Hill.
4. Rajiv's best friends are Gillian and Karla.
5. His pet isn't a dog, it's a parrot.
6. Karla is Rajiv's friend.
7. We aren't from York, we are from London.
8. Karla's hobby isn't football, it is wheelchair basketball.
9. I am good at wheelchair basketball.
10. She is happy about that.
11. Karla's pet is a rabbit.

S. 17 Words and Grammar: Vanessa

1. Vanessa is from Hendon – she isn't from Notting Hill.
2. She is eleven.
3. Her parents are Dan and Janet.
4. They aren't from India.
5. I'm not in a football team, but I am in a basketball team.
6. We are really good.
7. Are you in a football team?
8. Vanessa's hobbies are also music and dancing.
9. Kenny Hoover isn't Vanessa's pet.
10. She is an only child.
11. Vanessa's hair is red.

S. 18–19 Words and Grammar: What have they got?

a)
1. Megan, Priya
2. Megan
3. Megan, Mark
4. Megan, Leo

b)
1. Leo and Mark haven't got a computer.
2. Mark and Priya have got a rabbit.
3. I haven't got a parrot.
4. Leo has got a parrot, but he hasn't got a rabbit.
5. Lea and Priya have got bikes, but they haven't got skateboards.
6. Mark has got a bike, but he hasn't got a parrot.

c)
1. Who hasn't got a computer?
2. Who has got a rabbit?
3. Who hasn't got a parrot?
4. Who hasn't got a skateboard?
5. Who hasn't got a bike?

2 a) *Lösungsvorschlag*:
Priya hasn't got a skateboard, but she has got a bike.
Priya hasn't got a parrot, but she has got a rabbit.
Megan hasn't got a bike, but she has got a computer.
Mark hasn't got a computer, but he has got a bike.
Leo hasn't got a rabbit, but he has got a parrot.

b) *Lösungsvorschlag*:
Who has got a parrot? – Leo
Who has got a bike? – Leo, Mark, Priya
Who hasn't got a skateboard? – Leo, Priya
Who has got a computer? – Megan, Priya
Who hasn't got a rabbit? – Megan, Leo

S. 20–21 Words and Grammar: Welcome to Notting Hill

☆ ☾ a)

1. There is a bus.
2. There are children.
3. There are three shops.
4. There is a cat.

☾ b)

1. Yes, there is.
2. Yes, there are.
3. No, there isn't.
4. No, there aren't.

☼ c) *Lösungsvorschlag*:

1. There is a restaurant.
2. There are three cars.
3. There are pets.
4. There is a woman on a bike.
5. There is a parrot in Rajiv's room.

☼ d) 1. Is there a museum? – No, there isn't.
2. Is there a swimming pool? – No, there isn't.
3. Are there shops? – Yes, there are.
4. Is there a man with a guitar? – Yes, there is.
5. Is there a woman in a pink dress? – No, there isn't.

S. 22 Mediation: At the park

☆ 1J 2A 3D 4F 5E 6C 7G 8B 9I 10H

S. 22–23 Mediation: Say it in English, please!

☾ 1. I am … years old.
2. I have got a cat.
3. Have you got a brother?
4. I play the guitar.
5. Where is Holland Park?
6. Are you from Notting Hill?

S. 23 Mediation: Miles

☼ 1. Eine Katze ist entlaufen.
2. Miles ist sieben Jahre alt und schwarz-weiß. Er ist freundlich, immer hungrig und jagt gern Mäuse. Er wohnt in der Aubrey Road 65 hier in London.
3. Jederzeit unter 0364 907326 anrufen.

S. 24 Speaking: Talking about places

☆ ☾ ☼ 1. Rajiv's parrot is in Rajiv's room.
2. In the "Retro" shop you can buy clothes.
3. Rajiv's neighbour is reading a newspaper.
4. The new show is called "The Lion King".

Hier sind Beispiele für mögliche Aussagen:

☆ I can see a bus stop.
There is a red bus at the corner.
There are people in the picture.
I can also see animals.
I can see a woman on a bike.
There are cars on the street.
In the middle of the street are some people.
There are many shops.
There is a shop for animals.

☾ You can see many shops and people in the picture. In the middle of the street is one man with a purple t-shirt.
There are many shops. I can see the Notting Hill Grill, Retro clothing and a shop for pets.
I can see a mother and a child in a yellow car.

☼ There are many people with colourful clothes in the picture. In my area I can't see people with colourful clothes.
I can see a bus stop in the picture. We also have bus stops in my area.
I can see a man in the middle of the street. In my area we don't stop in the middle of the street.
There are many shops in the picture. There are a lot of shops in my area.

THEME 2: A fresh start

S. 25–26 Listening: Breakfast at school

☆ A healthy breakfast

☆ *Folgende Bilder musstest du markieren*:
2., 3., 5., 7., 8., 9.

☾ ☼ Emma: tea
Kelly: bananas
James: muesli, milk
Omar: orange juice, apples

☼ 1. James wants to have a Sunday breakfast.
2. The children don't have sausages because sausages are not healthy.
3. The children don't have fried eggs because you can't make fried eggs at school.

S. 27–28 Reading: Who is who?

☆ ☾ A2 B1 C3 D4

☾ ☼ 1. wrong 2. wrong 3. right 4. right

☼ 1. Walter's clothes are red and grey.
2. Janet has got blonde hair.
3. Peter's nose is long.
4. Peter is very tall and slim.

S. 28–29 Reading: Hendon School News

☆ 1. Laura Scott
2. Mr Kapoor
3. Mrs Lamont
4. James Liu

1. Mrs Lamont
2. Laura Scott
3. Mrs Lamont, James Liu
4. Laura Scott, Mr Kapoor, James Liu
5. Mr Kapoor, James Liu

6. James Liu
7. Mrs Lamont
8. Laura Scott
9. Mrs Lamont
10. Laura Scott

S. 30 Writing: Jonah's Saturday

Lösungsvorschlag:
On Saturdays Jonah gets up at 9 o'clock. First he walks the dog, then he meets friends and plays basketball. After that Jonah does his homework. In the afternoon he watches TV or he reads a book. Jonah goes to bed at 9:30.

S. 31 Anaya's Sunday

Lösungsvorschlag:
On Sundays Anaya has breakfast at 8:30. In the morning she plays tennis. She likes that a lot. Then she meets her friends. They go to the cinema or the library. Later Anaya plays with her cat. Her name is Milly. Then Anaya and her family have dinner.

S. 31 Your turn: At the weekend

Lösungsvorschlag:
On Saturdays I always get up late. I do my homework. After that I meet my friends. We go to the park or to the swimming pool. I have dinner with my family at 7 o'clock. After that I watch TV or read a book. On Sundays I often visit my cousins. That's great fun!

S. 32 Words and Grammar: Word lists

school things	body parts	breakfast things
ruler	face	muesli
chalk	neck	cornflakes
schoolbag	leg	toast
pencil case	back	bacon
exercise book	tooth	jam
pen	tummy	fried egg

Lösungsbeispiele:
school things: rubber, pencil
body parts: knee, foot
breakfast things: baked beans, sausages

people: parents, classmate, friend, sister, neighbour, teacher

Lösungsbeispiel: cousin

S. 33 Words and Grammar: The clock is ticking …

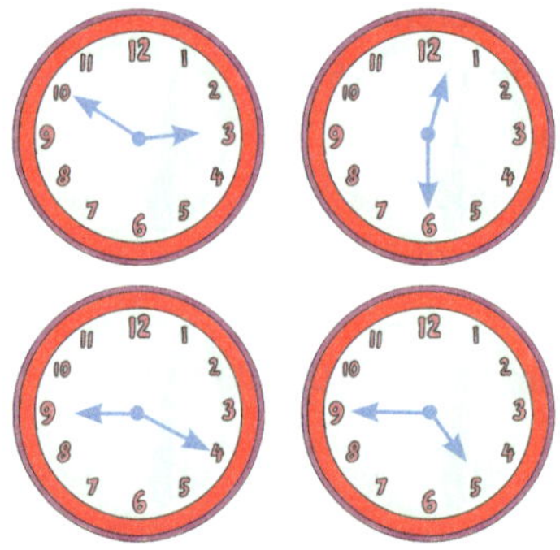

It's half past one. / It's one thirty.
It's twenty past five. / It's five twenty.
It's quarter to ten. / It's nine forty-five.

Lösungsvorschlag:

I have breakfast at seven o'clock.

I finish school at one fifteen.

S. 34–35 Words and Grammar: In the classroom

A8 B4 C1 D5 E7 F3 G2 H6

1. Look at the picture.
2. Listen to the CD.
3. Talk to your partner about the task.
4. Work in groups of four.
5. Write down the answer.
6. Turn to page 23.
7. Close the window, please.
8. Be quiet, please!

Don't talk to your neighbour.
Don't forget your homework.
Don't walk around.

S. 35 Words and Grammar: School rules

a) Be nice. Do your homework. Listen to the teachers. Wear the school uniform. Don't be late. Don't use mobiles at school. Don't eat during lessons. Don't play football in the classroom.

b) *Lösungsvorschlag*:
Don't forget your pen.
Eat a healthy lunch.

S. 36 Words and Grammar: The Millers' morning

☆ 1. Mr and Mrs Miller get up at 6:45.
2. Mr Miller makes breakfast.
3. Mrs Miller tells the children to get up.
4. They all have breakfast at 7:15.
5. Ben brushes his teeth at 7:45.
6. The children go to school at 8:15.
7. Mrs Miller goes to work at 8:20.

S. 36 Words and Grammar: The Lees' morning

☾ 1. gets	5. have
2. goes	6. brush
3. get	7. goes
4. make	8. leave

S. 37 Words and Grammar: The Jarvies' morning

☼ a) 1. Mr and Mrs Jarvies get up at 7 o'clock.
2. Mrs Jarvies makes breakfast.
3. Mr Jarvies plays with the dog.
4. Sam gets up at 7:15 in the morning.
5. They all have breakfast at 7:45 in the morning.
6. Sam washes his face and brushes his hair at 8 o'clock.
7. He also reads a comic.
8. Then he goes to school.
9. His parents leave the house at 8:30 in the morning.

b) Außer bei *he*, *she* und *it* (3. Person Singular) steht das Verb im *simple present* in der Grundform. bei *he*, *she* und *it* muss man ein -**(e)s** anhängen.

S. 38–39 Words and Grammar: Friends from London

☆ A4 B5 C8 D2 E1 F7 G3 H6

☾ 1. No, she isn't.	5. Yes, he does.
2. Yes, they are.	6. No, they don't.
3. Yes, they do.	7. Yes, she is.
4. No, they aren't.	8. No, she doesn't.

☼ 1. Do Ishan's parents speak Hindi? – Yes, they do.
2. Are Emily and Ishan friends? – Yes, they are.
3. Is Baxter Olivia's dog? – No, he isn't.
4. Does Chloe like music? – Yes, she does.
5. Is Ahmed a bad cook? – No, he isn't.
6. Does Olivia play football? – Yes, she does.

S. 39–40 Words and Grammar: 'A' or 'an'

☆ a dog	an idea
an animal	a classroom
a friend	an elephant
an answer	a teacher
a car	a pet

☾ an open door	a blue exercise book
a window	a clever answer
an old desk	an egg
a table	an English breakfast
a great idea	an old overhead projector
an interesting book	an orange scarf
an extra task	

☾ 'A' benutzt man, wenn das folgende Wort mit einem Konsonanten beginnt, 'an' bei einem Vokal.

☼ 1. Is this an English book? – No, it's a German book.
2. I have cornflakes and an apple for breakfast.
3. This isn't a new pencil. It's an old pencil.
4. Is this an exercise book? – Oh no, it's a textbook.
5. I have a great idea!
6. Do you have an answer for this question?
7. In school, we read an interesting book.

☼ 'A' benutzt man, wenn das folgende Wort mit einem Konsonanten beginnt, 'an' bei einem Vokal. Dabei kommt es auf die Aussprache an. ‚Uncle' fängt mit einem gesprochenen ‚u' (Vokal) an, ‚uniform' mit einem ‚j' (Konsonant). Bei ‚hobby' wird das ‚h' (Konsonant) gesprochen, bei ‚hour' ist es stumm.

S. 41 Mediation: Breakfast at a restaurant

☆ Ja. Es gibt Apfel, Orange und Grapefruit.
Ja, warme Milch haben sie auch.

☾ Es gibt auch Tee.
Sie haben Müsli.
Vollkornbrot gibt es leider nicht.

☼ Es gibt Schinkenspeck, Würstchen und Bohnen in Tomatensoße.
Ja, mit Marmelade oder Butter.
Ja, das gibt es.
Das gibt es auch.

S. 42–43 Speaking: On the way to school

Beispiele für die Unterhaltung:

☆ ☾ A: What time is it?
B: It's 8 o'clock.
A: Hurry up, please, we're late.

B: When does school start?
A: School starts at 10 past 8.
B: Have you got your English homework?
A: Yes, I have.
B: That's good.

A: What time is it?
B: It's 8:00 o'clock.
A: Hurry up, please, we're late.
B: When does school start?
A: School starts at 10 past 8.
B: Have you got your English homework?
A: Oh no, I haven't got my homework.
B: I can help you. What's for homework?
A: Homework is a text about my pet.
B: Have you got a pet?
A: No, I haven't. How can I say this in English?
B: You can write "I haven't got a pet".

S. 43 Speaking: Polly and Spot

Polly is a tall, slim monster. I can see five arms and two legs. Her ears are big and she has got a small nose and long, red hair. Her clothes are green, purple, blue and pink. She looks friendly.

Polly is a tall, slim monster. I can see five arms and two legs. Her ears are big and she has got a small nose and long, red hair. Her clothes are green, purple, blue and pink. She looks friendly. Spot is a small, blue monster. He has got four arms and two legs. I can see a big nose and big teeth, but his ears are small. His hair is green and his clothes are pink and red. He looks cool.

THEME 3: Free Time

S. 44–45 Listening: What can I do in my free time?

Die richtige Antwort ist „Hockey".

1. wrong
2. right
3. wrong
4. right
5. wrong
6. wrong

swimming: Monday at 4 o'clock
hockey: Tuesday at 5 o'clock
tennis: Wednesday at 3 o'clock
inline skating: Thursday in the afternoon
football: Friday at 6 o'clock

swimming: Monday at 4 o'clock, swimming pool at school
hockey: Tuesday at 5 o'clock on a playing field near Jacob's house
tennis: Wednesday at 3 o'clock on a tennis court
inline skating: Thursday in the afternoon in the park
football: Friday at 6 o'clock in the gym

S. 46 Reading: An event

1. horseback riding
2. Friday to Sunday, August 16th to 18th
3. at 10 am
4. at the playing field at Holland Park School
5. £12 per person/day
6. pizza, popcorn, chocolate, sandwiches, lemonade, tea, coffee and water

S. 47–48 Reading: Pets

Mike: I live on a farm and my pet is a chicken.
Alex: My pet has a big yellow beak and is called Kiki.
Lucy: I take my pet into the garden and she is a guinea pig.
Ross: My pet is big and likes carrots. She is a horse.
Sarah: My pet is big and is called Tigger.
Jane: My pet has four legs and white feet and he is a dog.

1. Tigger sleeps in a basket and eats cat food.
2. Bronwen is very tall and eats apples and carrots.
3. Arthur eats vegetables and lives with his brothers and sisters.
4. Fluffy lives in a small cage and eats spinach.
5. Kiki has a yellow beak and eats fruit all day.
6. Blacky sleeps outside and eats dog food and bones.
7. Blacky is nine years old and I take him for a walk every day.

S. 49–51 Writing: My (dream) pet

Lösungsvorschlag:
My pet is a dog. It is five years old and sleeps in a basket. It eats dog food and bones. It can roll over and jump very high. I take it for walks to my friend's house and to the park. It has white feet and friendly eyes.

Lösungsvorschlag:
My pet is a dog. It is five years old and sleeps in a basket. It eats dog food and bones. It can roll over and jump very high. I take it for to the park a walk or we play in the garden. It has white feet and friendly eyes. I love it because I can play with it and it runs very fast.

Lösungsvorschlag:
My favourite (dream) pet is a cat. It is big and can also speak. I can tell it everything. It is three years

old and has big blue eyes. She eats cat food but also vegetables and ice cream. It sleeps in a basket in her own room. We have breakfast and dinner together. I can take it to the park or we go to school together. I love it because it is my best friend and very funny!

S. 51 Writing: An exotic pet

☼ *Lösungsvorschlag*:

This is a crocopenguindinophant. Its name is Coco. Coco has a long green tail and a lot of colours. Ist favourite food ist pizza. It is very big but it can run fast. It helps me with my homework. It sleeps in an small house in our garden and plays with me every morning.

S. 52 Writing: What can they do?

☆ ☾

The boy can skate.
The boy can't play tennis.
The girl can't read.
The boy can sing.
The boy can do gymnastics.
The girl can't do karate.

☼ *Lösungmöglichkeiten:*

I can play football but I can't play basketball.
I can't swim but I can play tennis.
I can't jump high but I can run fast.

S. 53–54 Words and Grammar: Types of sport

☆ 1. go swimming
2. go skating
3. play basketball
4. ride a bike
5. go skiing
6. play hockey
7. play volleyball
8. do karate
9. do gymnastics
10. play football
11. ride a horse
12. play table tennis

☾ 1. go swimming
2. go skiing
3. play volleyball
4. do gymnastics
5. do karate
6. play basketball
7. play hockey
8. go skating
9. ride a horse
10. play football
11. ride a bike
12. play table tennis

☼ 1. go swimming in a pool
2. go skiing in the mountains
3. play volleyball in the gym
4. do gymnastics in your room
5. do karate in a sports hall
6. play basketball on a basketball field
7. play hockey on a hockey field
8. go skating in the park
9. ride a horse in the street
10. play football on a football field
11. ride a bike in the street
12. play table tennis in a gym

S. 54 Words and Grammar: Odd one out

☆ 1. library 2. winner 3. family 4. fantastic 5. today

The Holland Park team scores two goals and is the <u>winner</u> of the game.
David goes to the <u>library</u> on Thursday to read books.
"Josh, I want you to take the rubbish out <u>today</u>, not tomorrow."
The match between Holland Park and Hendon was absolutely <u>fantastic</u>.
We are a very active <u>family</u>.

S. 55 Words and Grammar: Matching

☾ a) 1. love – hate
2. can – can't
3. ask – answer
4. funny – boring
5. big – small
6. seller – customer
7. easy – difficult
8. am – pm
9. boy – girl
10. buy – sell
11. long – short
12. new – old

b) 1. seashell
2. football
3. classmate
4. postcard
5. playground
6. blackboard
7. weekend
8. something
9. lunchtime
10. goalkeeper

S. 56 Words and Grammar: Words, words, words …

☼ two sports you can do: gymnastics, karate
four question words: what, which, why, how
five words with "ea" *(möglich)*: easy, beach, teacher, beat, seashell, meal, teach reading
five adjectives *(möglich)*: boring, special, interesting, funny, easy, fantastic
five words with double consonants *(möglich)*: table tennis, sports hall, funny, well, till, winner, winning, swimming, collect, guess, odd, add, seller, call, will, cuddly toy, seashell, chill
rhymes: classmate – skate; see – free; game – aim; will – till; play – today

S. 57–59 Words and Grammar: What can or can't they do?

☆ 1. Sharon can swim but she can't run fast.
2. Josephine can do gymnastics but she can't play basketball.

3. Sheree can do karate but she can't play hockey.
4. Hoppity can eat carrots but he can't sleep in a basket.
5. Gillian and Vanessa can collect stickers but they can't ride a horse.
6. David and Rajiv can ride a bike but they can't feed pets.

1. Gillian and Vanessa can play football but they can't do gymnastics.
2. David can ski, but can't play table tennis.
3. Mrs Patel can cook but she can't skate.
4. Kenny can eat bones but he can't do tricks.
5. Karla can play basketball but she can't sing.

Lösungsvorschlag:
I can read a book but I can't cook a meal.
I can play hockey but I can't ride a horse.
I can't sing but I can play the guitar.

S. 59 Words and Grammar: Lots of question

1. Where can my new pet sleep?
2. What does my new pet eat?
3. Where can I take my new pet?
4. When do I have to walk my pet?
5. What tricks can my pet do?
6. Who can help me with my pet?
7. When do I take my pet to the vet?
8. Where can I play with my pet?

S. 60–61 Words and Grammar: Pets and hobbies

A3 B4 C2 D6 E1 F5

When does Kenny play? – Kenny plays at 5 pm.
What does Ruby eat? – Ruby eats oranges and apples.
Who feeds Ruby? – Rajiv feeds Ruby.
What does Kenny eat? – Kenny eats bones and dog food.
Who feeds Kenny? – The father feeds Kenny.

When does Kenny play? – Kenny plays at 5 pm.
When does Hoppity play? – Hoppity plays at 11 am.
What does Ruby eat? – Ruby eats oranges and apples.
Who feeds Ruby? – Rajiv feeds Ruby.
What does Kenny eat? – Kenny eats bones and dog food.
Who feeds Kenny? – The father feeds Kenny.
What does Hoppity eat? – Hoppity eats carrots and spinach.
Who feeds Hoppity? – Josh feeds Hoopity.

S. 61–62 Words and Grammar: Sentences and questions

1. Listen to the CD.
2. The book club meets on Mondays.
3. What do you need for your sport?
4. Prepare a presentation about your pet.
5. Turn the radio on and listen to the song.
6. Write about what you can or can't do!

1. Can your grandfather ski? – Yes, he can./No, he can't.
2. Can you ride a bike? – Yes, I can./No, I can't.
3. Can all your friends play hockey? – Yes, they can./No, they can't.
4. Can your parents drive a car? – Yes, they can./ No, they can't.
5. Can your teacher write the numbers from 1 to 100 in English? – Yes, she can./No, she can't.

1. When is the Karate Club?
2. How many free places are there?
3. Where is the Karate Club?
4. Who can join?
5. What do you wear?

S. 63–65 Mediation: At the market

Can you show me the poster of Tower Bridge, please?
Moment – hier ist es.
I like it very much! How much is it?
Es kostet neun Pfund fünfzig.
Dankeschön und hier ist dein Wechselgeld – 50 Pence.

Can you show me the poster of Tower Bridge, please?
Moment – hier ist es.
I don't like it. Can you show me the poster of Buckingham Palace, please?
Ja, natürlich.
I like it very much! How much is it?
Es kostet acht Pfund fünfundsiebzig.
I'll take it. Can you show me the poster of the race car, please?
Natürlich!
Oh, it's also fantastic! How much is it?
Es kostet fünf Pfund.
I only have twelve pound but I would like to buy both posters.
Ich kann dir beide Poster für 12 Pfund geben.
Vielen Dank und einen schönen Tag noch.

S. 66–67 Speaking: School clubs

Beispiel für die Unterhaltungen:

Partner/in A:

A: What club is it?
B: It's a Hockey Club. Who is welcome?
A: Everybody can come – girls and boys! What day is it?
B: It's on Monday. When does it start?
A: It starts at 3 pm.
B: Where is it?
A: It's on the sports field. Who is the teacher?
B: It's with Mr Morris.

Partner/in B:

B: What club is it?
A: It's a Drama Club. What do we do?
B: We do musicals. What day is it?
A: It's on Wednesday. What time does it start?
B: It starts at 4 pm. Where is the club?
A: It's in the school theatre. Who is the teacher?
B: It's with Mrs Johnson. Who is welcome?
A: Everybody can come, boys and girls, but you must be 13 or older

S. 67 Speaking: Rajiv and David

Rajiv and David can ski.
Rajiv can't skate but David can.
Rajiv can play hockey but David can't.
Rajiv and David can play football.
Rajiv can't play volleyball but David can.
Rajiv and David can't do gymnastics.

Lösungsbeispiel:
I can swim but I can't ski.
I can skate but I can't play hockey.
I can play football and volleyball but I can't do gymnastics.
I can't play table tennis and I can't do karate.

THEME 4: At home

S. 68–69 Listening: Nora's new room

Anzukreuzen sind der rote Schrank und der grau-schwarze Stuhl.

Folgende Wörter musstest du markieren:
lamp, bed, computer, cage, shelf, teddy bear

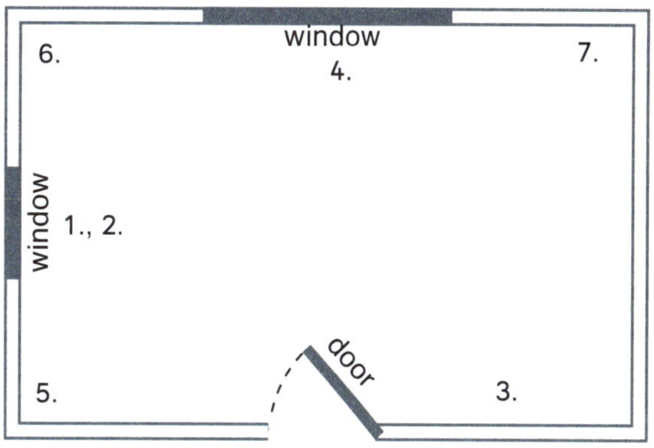

2. black and grey
3. in Nora's bed
4. on her desk
5. between her books on the new shelf
6. so her mother can't find it
7. after school

S. 70–72 Reading: Shopping for a sleepover

1. wrong
2. right
3. wrong
4. wrong
5. wrong
6. right

1. Josephine buys four pizzas.
2. Josephine wants to make fruit salad with bananas, kiwi and strawberries.
3. A bottle of orange juice costs 75 pence.
4. They want to eat crisps and chocolate with the movie.
5. The crisps cost 1 pound a bag.
6. Josephine pays 10 pounds 96 pence altogether.

A4 B6 C1 D2 E3 F5

1. Vanessa and Sheree
2. pizza
3. four pizzas
4. two sausage and two extra cheese pizzas
5. fruit salad
6. two pound(s)
7. apple juice, orange juice and water
8. two bottles
9. 75 pence
10. ten pounds and 96 pence
11. nine pound(s) and four pence

S. 73–75 Writing: Sharon's week

☆ ☾ ☼ On Tuesdays she never does the cooking at home.
On Wednesdays Sharon often plays tennis with her mother.
On Thursdays Sharon always watches TV.
On Fridays she often tidies her room.
On Saturdays she sometimes goes for a walk with her father.
On Sundays Sharon usually stays in bed and reads a book.

☼ *Lösungsbeispiele*:
On Mondays I usually go to the book club in the library after school.
On Tuesdays I often visit my grandmother.
On Wednesdays I often play hockey with my friends.
On Thursdays I always do my homework.
On Fridays I sometimes go shopping with my best friend.
On Saturdays I always clean my room and sometimes I watch a film with friends.
On Sundays I sometimes have a big breakfast with my family and stay in bed.

☼ *Lösungsbeispiel*:
My favourite day of the week is Saturday because I have a lot of time to play with my friends and we can go to the park together.

S. 76 Writing: Who does what?

Lösungsvorschlag:
☆ She always tidies her room. Josephine also always tidies her room and sometimes she takes out the rubbish. But she never empties the dishwasher.

☾ ☼ She always tidies her room. Mr Batson sometimes takes out the rubbish. Mrs Batson usually cleans the kitchen. Josephine always tidies her room and sometimes she takes out the rubbish. But she never empties the dishwasher.

☼ My parents usually go to the supermarket. Sometimes my mother works in the garden. My sister and me often help her. My brother, my sister and me always tidy our rooms. My brother never empties the dishwasher. My mother tidies the living room and the kitchen. My father sometimes takes out the rubbish.

S. 77–78 Words and grammar: What is in my room?

☆
1. shelf
2. computer
3. lamp
4. desk
5. chair
6. pillow
7. duvet
8. posters
9. wardrobe
10. cage
11. bed
12. TV

☾
1. posters
2. bed
3. pillow
4. duvet
5. TV
6. cage
7. guitar
8. wardrobe
9. lamp
10. computer
11. desk
12. chair

☼ a) shelf, computer, lamp, desk, chair, pillow, duvet, posters, wardrobe, cage, bed, TV
b) *Mögliche Antworten:*
The lamp is on the desk. The chair is next to the desk. The wardrobe is behind the desk. The skateboard is under the bed. The guitar is next to the wardrobe. The shelf is above the bed. The books are on the shelf. The guinea pigs are in the cage. The posters are above the bed. Pillow and duvet are in the bed. A little cuddle bear sits on the shelf.

S. 79–80 Words and grammar: Food and drink

☆ **fruit:** apples, bananas
vegetables: carrots, beans, tomatoes
drinks: lemonade, milk, orange juice, water
sweet snacks: biscuits, cake, chocolate, cookies
other: cheese, crisps, sandwiches, sausages

☾ **sweet snacks:** biscuits, cake, chocolate, ice cream
fruit: apples, bananas
vegetables: beans, carrots, spinach, tomatoes
drinks: lemonade, milk, orange juice, water
other: cheese, crisps, sausages, sandwiches

☼ **sweet snacks:** biscuits, cake, chocolate, ice cream
fruit: apples, bananas
vegetables: beans, carrots, spinach, tomatoes
drinks: lemonade, milk, orange juice, water
party food: cheese, crisps, sausages, sandwiches

S. 80–82 Words and grammar: Jobs at home

☆ ☾ ☼
1. do the cooking
2. do the shopping
3. make my bed
4. clean the bathroom
5. vacuum the floor

6. feed the pets
7. tidy my room
8. take out the rubbish
9. look after the children
10. empty the dishwasher

Lösungsvorschlag:
1. vacuum the floor, empty the dishwasher, make the bed, do the cooking, clean the bathroom
2. chocolate, crisps, lemonade, sandwiches, a film
3. tidy – untidy; boring – interesting; turn out – turn on; in front of – behind; get out – get in; always – never; evening – morning; dinner – breakfast

S. 82–84 Words and grammar: Pronouns and possessives

1. Charlie lives in Hendon. He has got three pets. His pets are goldfish.
2. Vanessa and Gillian are friends. They play football together. Their team has got ten players and a goalkeeper.
3. Josephine likes to play Hockey. She is in the hockey club at school. Her sister Sharon is also in the team.
4. My friends and I like to swim. We go to the pool every day. Our swimming teacher is Mr Hacker.
5. At home my brother and I have jobs to do. We clean the kitchen and tidy our rooms.
6. Rajiv has got a pet. He feeds his parrot every day and cleans the cage.
7. Mrs Marshall likes to go shopping. She buys fruit and vegetables for her family.
8. Mr Patel and his son have a hobby. They like fast cars.
9. David likes to eat sandwiches. He makes his lunch when he comes from school.
10. My family and I go shopping every weekend. We buy everything we need for the weekend. Our kitchen is a busy place.

words for a girl: she, her
words for a boy: he, his
words for two people or a group: they, their
words for you and your family, you and your friends, you and … : we, our

S. 85–86 Words and grammar: What do the children do at home?

1. Josh always vacuums the floor.
2. Gillian sometimes makes her bed.
3. Rajiv often tidies his room.
4. David usually does the washing up.
5. Vanessa never cleans the kitchen.
6. Charlie sometimes empties the dishwasher.
7. Josephine usually does the cooking.

S. 86–88 Words and grammar: Who does it belong to?

1. This is Charlie's computer.
2. This is Gillian's cat.
3. These are Vanessa's marbles.
4. This is Sharon's seashell.
5. These are Mrs Marshall's books.
6. These are Mr Patel's sandwiches.
7. This is Rajiv's bike.
8. This is David's pencil case.
9. This is Ruby's cage.
10. This is Anna Coleman's car.

1. Josh's rabbit ist brown and white.
2. Karla's basketball ist new.
3. Mr Batson's inline skates are new.
4. Dan's favourite football team ist Chelsea.
5. Anna Coleman's new tennis partner is Mrs Batson.
6. David's new mobil phone is mall.
7. Mahmut's new guitar is brown.
8. Vanessa's room ist untidy.
9. Eleanor's hot chocolate is sweet.
10. Sheree's ghost stories are spooky.
11. Tom's marbles are colourful.
12. Diego's horse ist black and grey.

S. 89–91 Mediation: Skyping with Grandma

Hi Grandma, Tom says: "I never tidy my room."
Grandma sagt, dass du dein Zimmer aufräumen kannst.
Tom says: „Tristan always takes out the rubbish."
Dad does the cooking every day.
Mum always cleans the bathroom.
Und was machst du, Tom?
I sometimes make my bed.

Hi Grandma, Tom says: "I never tidy my room."
Grandma sagt, dass du dein Zimmer aufräumen kannst.
Tom says: „Tristan always takes out the rubbish."
Dad does the cooking every day and always does the washing up.
Mum always cleans the bathroom, vacuums the floor and cleans the kitchen.
Und was machst du, Tom?
I sometimes make my bed and I help dad with the shopping.

S. 92–93 Speaking: My room and your room

Mögliche Beschreibungen:

Partner A: On the left side is a brown wardrobe. In the wardrobe there are clothes. Behind the wardrobe there is a white desk. On the desk is a computer. Next to the desk is a brown chair. Above the computer is a foodball poster. There is a shelf above the desk. It is beside of the poster. There are books in the shelf. Under the shelf is a bed. The pillow is yellow, the duvet orange. Above the bed are posters. Next to the bed is a big lamp.

Partner B: On the left side is a red desk. The computer is on the desk. Next to the desk is a red chair. Above the computer are two posters. Behind the desk is a big green wardrobe. On the right side is a red bed. There are clothes on the bed. Next to the bed is a big lamp. Beside the wardrobe and above the bed is a shelf. There are books in the shelf.

THEME 5: Day by day

S. 94–95 Listening: Nadiya's favourite school day

Folgende Wörter musstest du markieren:

1. Tuesday
2. drama, music

Folgenden Buchstaben musstest du abhaken: D

Folgende Wörter musstest du abhaken:

Food and drink in the canteen: sandwiches, pizza, fish and chips, water, lemonade, chocolate ice creme

Nadiya eats: fish and chips, salad, lemonade, chocolate ice cream

1. Usually School starts at 8 o'clock.
2. On Tuesdays, Nadiya goes to school by car.
3. Nadyia's favourite teacher is Mrs King.
4. She goes to school at half past eight.
5. Daniel's second lesson is English.
6. Daniel likes music because they can sing songs and listen to pop music.
7. Nadiya thinks geography in the afternoon is terrible.
8. Her favourite lesson is music.
9. At home Nadiya cooks her favourite meal for dinner.
10. School ends at half past four.

S. 96–98 Reading: David's email

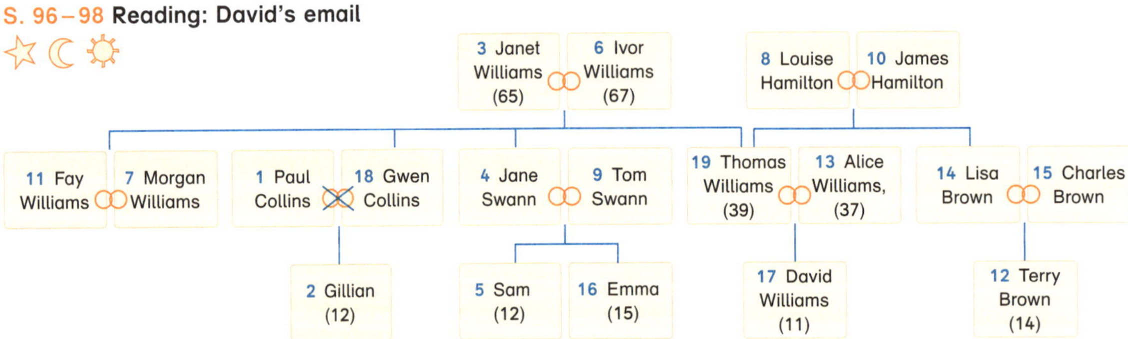

1. wrong
2. right
3. wrong
4. wrong
5. wrong
6. wrong
7. right
8. wrong
9. right
10. right

1. Emma
2. Gillian
3. Jane and Tom
4. Janet Williams
5. Lisa Brown
6. Sam
7. Sam
8. David and his family
9. Emma
10. Lisa Brown
11. Anna Coleman
12. Alice Williams

S. 99 Writing: Gillian's school day

☆ ☾ ☼ *Lösungsvorschlag*:

A5 B2 C1 D6 E4 F3

Lösungsvorschlag:

☆ Every school day, Gillian gets up at 7 o'clock. Then she has breakfast with coffee, orange juice and some toast. In the afternoon she often plays games with her friends or family. In the evening she eats a fresh salad.

☾ Every school day, Gillian gets up at 7 o'clock. Then she has breakfast with coffee, orange juice and some toast. After breakfast Gillian goes to school by bus. In the afternoon after school she plays some games with her friends or family. Sometimes she also listens to music. In the evening she makes a fresh salad.

☼ Every school day, Gillian gets up at 7 o'clock. Then she has breakfast with coffee, orange juice and some toast. After breakfast Gillian goes to school by bus. In the afternoon after school she plays some games with her friends or family. Sometimes she also listens to music. In the evening she makes a fresh salad for dinner. At 8 o'clock she has dinner with her family. After that she goes to bed.

S. 100 Writing: Your dream school day

☆ My dream school day starts at 10 o'clock in the morning. I go to school by plane. My subjects are cooking, playing games, listening to music and singing together in class. My school day finishes at one o'clock in the afternoon.

☾ My dream school day starts at 10 o'clock in the morning. I go to school by plane. My subjects are cooking, playing games, listening to music and singing together in class. In the breaks my friend and I play together. At lunchtime I have some candy and biscuits and pink lemonade. My school day finishes at one o'clock in the afternoon.

☼ My dream school day starts at 10 o'clock in the morning. In every classroom there is a swimming pool and there are some couches. We start with a big breakfast. I get to school by plane. My subjects are cooking, playing games, listening to music and singing together in class. We have lots of breaks. In the breaks my friends and I play together. At lunchtime I have some candy and biscuits and pink lemonade. My school day finishes at one o'clock in the afternoon.

S. 101 Words and grammar: Odd one out

☆ 1. July
2. cake
3. on foot
4. registration
5. torch
6. balloon
7. break
8. schoolbag

S. 101 Words and grammar: What is it?

☾ ☼ 1. canteen
2. schoolbag
3. uniform
4. registration
5. PE
6. break
7. ICT
8. music

S. 102–103 Words and grammar: Juliana's birthday

☆ 1. 03/02: Mum
2. 30/08: Olivia
3. 13/07 Juliana
4. 15/04 David
5. 31/10: Dad
6. 22/05: Adnan

☆

January	February	March
2nd Carrie	3rd Mum	30th Abdul
April	**May**	**June**
15th David	22nd Adnan	3rd Fluffy
July	**August**	**September**
13th me ☺	30th Olivia	
October	**November**	**December**
31st Dad	12th Jason	

☾ 1. David
2. Mum
3. Dad
4. Juliana (me)
5. Olivia
6. Adnan

☾ 1. 01/01 *oder* 1st January
2. 09/03 *oder* 9th March
3. 23/06 *oder* 23rd June

☼ 1. the sixteenth day of the first month
2. the twenty-ninth day of the eighth month
3. the eighth day of the seventh month

S. 103–104 Words and grammar: A birthday party

☆ 1. candles
2. picnic
3. balloons
4. presents
5. calendar
6. dancing

☾ *Lösungsvorschlag:*

A7 B5 C1 D2 E4 F3 G6

☼ 1. sing "Happy Birthday!"
2. write a birthday card
3. do magic tricks
4. open presents
5. have a picnic
6. make a cake
7. blow out candles

S. 104–106 Words and grammar: What are they doing?

☆ ☾ ☼ *Lösungsvorschlag*:
1. Erin is getting up.
2. She is walking to school.
3. The pupils are listening to the teacher.
4. Tom isn't feeding the cats.
5. The family is having dinner.
6. The boys aren't playing football.

☼ 7. Janet is playing video games.
8. Thomas is sleeping on the couch.
9. David is not washing the dishes.

S. 107 Words and grammar: Gillian's school day

☆ ☾ ☼ 1. When does Gillian get up?
2. What does she want for breakfast?
3. Where is her schoolbag?
4. What are her favourite lessons?
5. How many pupils are in Gillian's class?

☾ ☼ 6. Who is her best friend at school?
7. How does she get to school?
8. When does her school day finish?
9. When do Gillian and her friends have lunch?
10. Why does Gillian hurry home?

☼ 1. Who is Rajiv's friend?
2. Where do the friends meet at school every day?
3. When does school start?
4. What are you having for lunch today?
5. How do you get to school every day?

S. 108–109 Mediation: Can you help out?

☆ ☾ ☼ 1. Er fragt, ob er uns helfen kann.
2. My cousin is looking for a green T-shirt.
3. Die grünen T-Shirts sind da drüben.
4. Have you got this green T-shirt in small?
5. How much is the T-shirt?
6. Das kostet 10 Pfund fünfzig.

☼ 7. Here are fifteen pounds.
8. Und hier sind vier Pfund fünfzig zurück.

S. 110–112 Speaking: On the way to school

☆ *Lösungsvorschlag*:

A: When does the first lesson end?
B: It ends at 9:20 am. When does the second lesson start?
A: It starts at 9:45 am. When does the third lesson start?
B: The third lesson starts at 11:30 am. When does the fourth lesson end?
A: It ends at 3:10 pm. What is the third lesson on Mondays?
B: It's German. What is the first lesson on Tuesdays?
A: It's English. What is the last lesson on Tuesdays?
B: It's PE. What is the last lesson on Thursdays?
A: It's ICT. What is the second lesson on Wednesdays?
B: It's RE. What is the second lesson on Fridays?
A: It's music.

☾ ☼ *Lösungsvorschlag*:

A: When does the first lesson end?
B: It ends at 9:20 am. When does it start?
A: It starts at 8 o'clock. When does the second lesson start?
B: It starts at quarter to ten. When does it end?
A: It ends at 11:05 am. When does the third lesson end?
B: It ends at 12:50 pm. When does it start?
A: It starts at half past eleven. When does the last lesson start?
B: It starts at ten to two. When does it end?
A: It ends at 3:10 pm. What is the third lesson on Monday?
B: The third lesson on Monday is German. What is the second lesson?
A: The second lesson on Monday is English. What is the second lesson on Tuesday?
B: On Tuesday the second lesson is geography. What is the first lesson?
A: It's English. What is the last lesson?
B: It's PE. What is the third lesson on Tuesday?
A: The third lesson is maths. What is the second lesson on Wednesday?
B: The second lesson is RE. What is the first lesson on Wednesday?
A: The first lesson on Wednesday is science. What is the first lesson on Thursday?
B: The first lesson on Thursday is maths. What is the third lesson on Thursday?
A: The third lesson on Thursday is ICT. What is third lesson on Friday?
B: It's drama. What is the second lesson on Friday?
A: It's music.

☼ B: How many courses do the students have?
A: They have twelve courses. How often do they start at 8 o'clock?
B: They start at 8 o'clock every morning. When does school end at 3:10 pm?
A: It ends at 3:10 pm on Tuesday.

THEME 6: Out and about

S. 113–114 Listening: A family weekend at the farm

Mum: 

Dad:  

Allyson: 

Josephine: 

Liam: 

1. The farm is close to London.
2. Allyson rode a horse.
3. They went home at half past eleven on Sunday morning.

1B 2A 3C 4C 5A 6B

Lösungsvorschlag:

1 Mr and Mrs Buchanan wanted to go to the beach or to visit Allyson's aunt in Manchester.
2. The family looked at the animals.
3. The boy fell in the pond.
4. The Buchanans didn't have much time because they wanted to go home before lunch.

S. 115–117 Reading: Holidays at the summer camp

Folgende Bilder musstest du abhaken:

1., 3., 5., 6., 7., 8., 9.

A9 B1 C7 D4 E5 F10 G3 H6 I8 J2

1. B 2. B 3. B 4. C 5. A 6. C 7. A 8. A

S. 118 Writing: Things to do on a farm

Lösungsvorschlag:

You can do a lot of things on a farm. I'd like to ride a horse because I love horses. I don't want to feed the pigs because I think that's boring. You can also ride on a tractor. I'd like to have a picnic on the farm too.

Lösungsvorschlag:

You can do a lot of things on a farm. I don't want to ride a horse because I don't like horses. But I want to feed the pigs because they are funny and cute. It's fun to ride on a tractor. You can do it there with the farmer. I'd also like to have a picnic on the farm.

Lösungsvorschlag:

You can do a lot of things on a farm. I want to ride a horse because I love horses. I don't want to feed the pigs because I think that's boring. But it's fun to ride on a tractor with the farmer! I'd also like to have a picnic on the farm. And I want to see the sheep. I'd like to take photos of everything on the farm.

S. 119 Writing: My last summer holidays

Lösungsvorschlag:

In the last summer holidays I visited my grandparents in the south of Germany. I was there for two weeks and had a great time. We often played in the garden and when it was rainy I played card games with my grandparents. Back home I met with friends.

Lösungsvorschlag:

In the last summer holidays I went to Spain. I spent three weeks there and had a great time. My family and I visited some friends. We went shopping in Madrid. We often went to the beach and played in the sand or went swimming. When I was back home I met my friends. I really liked my summer holidays.

Lösungsvorschlag:

In the last summer holidays I went to Spain. I spent three weeks there and had a great time. My family and I visited some friends in Madrid. We also went shopping there. We stayed in a hotel near the beach. So I played in the sand and went swimming very often. When I was back home I met my friends. We went to the cinema and went skateboarding. I really liked my summer holidays.

S. 120 Words and grammar: Words, words, words

Lösungsbeispiele ab Zeile 5

animals	places	people
sheep	farm	biker
bull	field	beginner
cow	castle	farmer
chicken	bridge	professional

Lösungsbeispiele ab Zeile 5

actions	places	people
laugh	farm	biker
brush	field	professional
cross	information stand	keeper
search	kitchen	teacher
ride	library	parents

Lösungsbeispiele ab Zeile 5

nouns	verbs	adjectives
holiday	move	rainy
bridge	shout	high
tractor	land	excited
month	wave	surprised
plane	cross	sunny
autumn	search	silly
membership	hire	true
pair	offer	brilliant

S. 121–122 Words and grammar: Opposites

out – in	cold – hot
late – early	winter – summer
down – up	false – true

out – in	winter – summer
beginner – professional	down – up
cold – hot	false – true
exciting – boring	indoor – outdoor
late – early	on the left – on the right
rainy – sunny	yesterday – tomorrow

out – in	false – true
cold – hot	indoor – outdoor
late – early	on the left – on the right
winter – summer	yesterday – tomorrow
down – up	near – far

Lösungsbeispiele für Ergänzungen:

brilliant – silly	beginner – professional

S. 122–123 Words and grammar: Phrases

1. feed the pigs
2. have a good time
3. pick something up
4. have a picnic
5. get on well
6. have a crush on somebody
7. be on holiday
8. wave at/to somebody
9. ride on a tractor
10. eat spaghetti
11. go on holiday
12. open a door

1. feed the chicken
2. ride on a tractor
3. work on the field
4. go to the hen house
5. have a picnic
6. help the farmer
7. cross a bridge
8. swim in the pond
9. meet the animals
10. take photos

S. 123–124 Words and grammar: Gillian's weekend

Last weekend Gillian and her family went to a farm in Wales. There were ducks, chicken, sheep, goats, cows and a bull on the farm. In the afternoon Gillian and her family helped the farmer. Gillian worked with the farmer in the fields. After the work was finished, Gillian rode a pony. At 6 o'clock in the evening the farmer invited the Collins family to have dinner with him. What an interesting day!

Last weekend Gillian and her family went to a farm in Wales. There were ducks, chickens, sheep, goats, cows and a bull on the farm. At 1 pm the Collinses had a picnic in the picnic area. In the afternoon Gillian helped the farmer. Anna Coleman and Mrs Collins fed the animals. Gillian worked with the farmer in the fields. After the work was finished Gillian rode a pony. She really loved that. At 6 o'clock in the evening the farmer invited the Collinses to have dinner with him. What an interesting day!

Last weekend Gillian and her family went to a farm in Wales. They started at 10 am in Notting Hill. After two hours they arrived at the farm. The farmer showed them all the animals. There were ducks, chickens, sheep, goats, cows and a bull on the farm. At 1 pm the Collinses had a picnic in the picnic area. In the afternoon Gillian helped the farmer. Anna Coleman and Mrs Collins fed the animals. Gillian worked with the farmer in the fields. After the work was finished, Gillian rode a pony. She really loved that. At 6 o'clock in the evening the farmer invited the Collinses to have dinner with him. What an interesting day!

S. 125 Words and grammar: What did you do last week?

Lösungsvorschlag:
Last week on Monday I went to school. On Tuesday I read a book. I watched TV on Thursday. Last week on Friday I visited friends.

Last week on Wednesday I played hockey. Last week on Saturday I had dinner with my family.

S. 126 Words and grammar: Just a normal day

☆ ☾ ☼ *Lösungsvorschlag*:

1. Rajiv and Gillian are riding on a tractor.
2. The boy is playing tennis.
3. David and Charlie are playing computer games.
4. Sally is brushing her teeth.
5. Lisa is trying to reading a book.
6. David is sleeping.

S. 127–128 Mediation: At the holiday camp

☆ ☾ ☼ *Lösungsvorschlag*:

Lieber Niclas,
ich habe folgende Aktivitäten herausgefunden, die wir im Feriencamp machen könnten:
Man kann einen Gitarrenkurs machen. Er findet jeden Dienstag und Donnerstag um 15 Uhr in der Camp Cafeteria statt.
Wer Karten- oder Brettspiele mag, kann montags zum Spielabend gehen. Er findet in Raum 12 um 19 Uhr statt. Man kann seine eigenen Lieblingsspiele mitbringen.
Montags um 10 Uhr beginnt das Basketballtraining auf dem Spielfeld. Am Ende des Camps gibt es ein Basketballspiel und die Gewinner bekommen einen tollen Preis!
Wenn man gern fotografiert, kann man am Fotografie-Kurs teilnehmen. Man lernt dort, gute Fotos zu machen. Es findet jeden Sonntagmorgen um 9:00 Uhr in der Haupthalle statt. Man muss seine eigene Kamera mitbringen.
Wer gern backt, kann am Backwettbewerb teilnehmen und seinen Lieblingskuchen und Lieblingskekse backen. Der beste Kuchen und die besten Kekse erhalten als Preis ein Kochbuch. Der Wettbewerb findet am ersten Camp-Samstag um 15 Uhr in der Camp-Küche statt.
Ich freue mich schon sehr auf das Camp!

S. 129 Speaking: At the funny farm

☆ ☾ ☼ *Hier sind Beispiele für mögliche Aussagen:*

I can see a pig with a camera. It is taking pictures of the funny farm. There is a bull wearing a blue t-shirt. He also has a ring in his nose. A dog is eating a banana and two rabbits are dancing. There is a black and white horse at a table eating with the farmer. Three chicken are riding a horse and two goats are riding a bike. The sheep are playing football.

☼ I would play football and dance with the rabbits. I'd also like to have a picnic together with the horse and the farmer.

S. 130 Speaking: Making plans for the weekend

☆ ☾ ☼ A: Hello.

B: Hi, great to hear from you! How are you?

A: I'm fine. I'm looking forward to the weekend on the city farm!

B: I'm looking forward to it, too. When are we going to the farm?

☾ A: We are going to be at your place at 3 pm. What are we going to do on the farm?

B: What about feeding the animals, having a picnic and riding a horse.

A: Those are great ideas. What about riding on a tractor?

B: That sounds good!

☼ A: In case the weather is bad on the weekend we play card games or draw animals.

B: Yes, and we can bake a cake or watch a film.

A: I have to go for dinner now. Goodbye!

B: See you soon!

Texte zu den Hörverstehensaufgaben auf der CD

Track	Theme	Titel	Spielzeit
1	Theme 1: People and places	Meet Greg and Mathilda	1:07
2	Theme 1: People and places	Meet Balraj and Fiona	1:12
3	Theme 2: A fresh start	Breakfast at school	2:13
4	Theme 3: Free time	What can I do in my free time	1:57
5	Theme 4: At home	Nora's new room	1:46
6	Theme 5: Day by day	Nadiya's favourite school day	2:50
7	Theme 6: Out and about	A family weekend at the farm	3:17

THEME 1: People and places

zu S. 6: Meet Greg and Mathild

Greg: Hi, I'm Greg Miller. I live in Hendon. I'm eight. I have got a sister. Her name is Jenna. She is six years old and she is in a wheelchair. My mother lives with us, but my father lives in York. We have got a dog. His name is Barker. I play the guitar and I love football.

Mathilda: Hi, I'm Matilda Balinski. I'm nine and I live in Hendon. I have got a brother and a sister, but I haven't got a pet. I like to play the guitar and tennis, but I don't like dancing. My favourite food is pizza. I haven't got a bike, but I have got a skateboard.

zu S. 7: Meet Balraj and Fiona

Balraj: Hi, I'm Balraj. What's your name?
Fiona: My name is Fiona. Are you from London?
Balraj: Yes, I am. But my parents are from India. What about you?
Fiona: I'm from London, too. I live here with my Mum. My father lives in Birmingham.
Balraj: How old are you, Fiona?
Fiona: I'm twelve. How old are you?
Balraj: I'm twelve, too. I've got a sister. She is eight. Have you got any brothers or sisters?
Fiona: No, I haven't. But I've got a cat! Her name is Miss Kitty!
Balraj: That's a very nice name. I have got goldfish. They haven't got names.
Fiona: Do you play football, Balraj?
Balraj: No, I don't like football. I play basketball and I love music.
Fiona: I play football. I'm in a team and we are really good! And I love music, too.
Balraj: Let's go to the music shop.
Fiona: Great idea!

THEME 2: A fresh start

zu S. 25-26: Breakfast at school

Emma: Breakfast at school is a great idea!
Kelly: It is! What do we want to eat?
James: What about a big Sunday breakfast? I love that!
Omar: I don't think that is a good idea. A big Sunday breakfast is not healthy.
Kelly: You're right, Omar. I would like a healthy breakfast. Emma, what about you?
Emma: I think so, too. James, are you OK with that?
James: Hmm. Well, OK.
Emma: Great! A healthy breakfast it is! What do we need?
James: What about sausages?
Omar: Sausages are not healthy, silly! We don't need sausages! We need muesli and fresh fruit and so on. I can bring some juice.
Kelly: Let's make a list. Omar, can you bring some orange juice?
Omar: Yes, I can. And I can bring some apples.
Kelly: Good. Let me write that down. Omar brings orange juice and apples. What about muesli?
James: I can bring that. And I can bring some eggs. Then we can make fried eggs.
Emma: I don't think you can make fried eggs at school.
James: Ok. So no fried eggs then. What about milk for the muesli?
Emma: Yes, that is a good idea. Kelly, write it down, please. James brings muesli and milk. And
I can bring tea.
Kelly: Got it. Emma brings tea. I can bring some bananas. Do we need anything else?
Emma: No, that's it. See you tomorrow.
Kelly: Perfect! See you!
Omar: Bye!
James: Bye!

THEME 3: Free time

zu S. 44-45: What can I do in my free time?

Eleanor: Hello, Jacob, how are you?
Jacob: Hi, Eleanor, I'm fine and you?
Eleanor: I'm OK but I have a big problem.
Jacob: Can I help?
Eleanor: Yeah, maybe. I need to find something to do in my free time. I want to do some kind of sport, but I don't know what.
Jacob: Well, I can tell you what I do in my free time. On Mondays I swim in the pool at school at
4 o'clock.
Eleanor: I'm not very good at swimming, Jacob.
Jacob: OK, what about hockey? I play hockey on a playing field near my house on Tuesdays.
Eleanor: What time do you start?
Jacob: We start at 5 o'clock.
Eleanor: Maybe I can play hockey! I can run really fast! The time is good, too because my library club ends at 4 o'clock.
Jacob: That sounds good. We need fast players in the team.
Eleanor: What about Wednesdays? What do you do then?
Jacob: I play tennis on a tennis court. We start at 3 o'clock.
Eleanor: I don't like tennis.
Jacob: On Thursdays I go inline skating in a park with my friends in the afternoon.
Eleanor: That doesn't work for me. I don't have skates. What else do you do?
Jacob: I play football in a boys' team at 6 o'clock in the gym on Fridays.
Eleanor: Does your sports club have a girls' team, too?
Jacob: Yes, it does, but the girls' team plays on Tuesdays at 3 o'clock.
Eleanor: That's not a good time for me but hockey sounds good!
Jacob: Hockey is a lot of fun and you don't need anything to play. You can use the club's sticks and balls.
Eleanor: Sounds great! See you at the playing field on Tuesday!

THEME 4: At home

zu S. 68-69: Nora's new room

Nora: Hi, Anthony.
Anthony: Hello, Nora. How are you?
Nora: I'm great, thank you! I've got a new room. It's really cool!
Anthony: Fantastic! Tell me all about it.
Nora: OK. I've got a new desk and chair. The desk is red, my favourite colour. The chair is black and grey. They are in front of the small window, on the left in my room.
Anthony: Wow, that's nice!
Nora: I also have a new red wardrobe. It's next to the door on the right. My bed is under the big window.
Anthony: And what else do you have?
Nora: My new shelf is next to my desk on the left. There's a lamp next to my desk on the right. The cage with my parrot is in the corner of my room next to my bed on the right.
Anthony: Where is your computer?
Nora: On my desk.
Anthony: And where is your teddy bear?
Nora: He's in my bed, of course!
Anthony: And where do you put your chocolate so your mother can't find it?
Nora: *(laughs)* Between my books on my new shelf.
Anthony: Your room is really nice. Can I visit you tomorrow and see it?
Nora: Yes of course! You can come after school.
Anthony: Great, Nora! Talk to you later. Bye!
Nora: Bye, Anthony!

THEME 5: Day by day

zu S. 94-95: Nadiya's favourite school day

Nadiya: Hello, Daniel, how are you?
Daniel: Hi, Nadiya, I'm fine, thanks.
Nadiya: I'm so happy! It's Tuesday – my favourite school day.
Daniel: No, I don't like Tuesdays. They're boring. Thursday is my favourite school day.
Nadiya: Tuesdays are super! School starts half an hour later – at half past eight. So I go to school with my mum – by car.
Daniel: Oh really? That's great!
Nadiya: My first lesson is drama. That's really cool.
Daniel: I hate drama! But English in the second lesson is OK.
Nadiya: That's right. And after English we have my favourite lesson of the week: music.
Daniel: I like music because we can sing songs and listen to pop music.
Nadiya: But I don't like geography in the afternoon. It's terrible.
Daniel: Yes, that's right. Nadiya, what club do you go to today?
Nadiya: On Tuesdays I always read books in the school library. I like the book club because Mrs King, my favourite teacher, talks about some interesting books for children. At half past four I go home and cook my favourite meal for dinner.
Narrator: At 12:40 in the canteen:
Nadiya: Let's see what they've got in the canteen today: sandwiches, pizza and fish and chips. As dessert they've got biscuits and chocolate ice cream. Today's drinks are water and lemonade.
Daniel: Yes, pizza, I love it!
Kitchen help: Hello, what can I get you?
Daniel: I'd like some pizza, lemonade and some biscuits, please.
Kitchen help: Here you are. And for you?
Nadiya: I would like fish and chips and a salad, please.
Kitchen help: Would you like a drink too?
Nadiya: Yes, a lemonade, please.
Kitchen help: Anything else?
Nadiya: Some chocolate ice cream, please.
Kitchen help: Here you are.
Nadiya and Daniel: Thanks. Bye!

THEME 6: Out and about

zu S. 113-114: A family weekend at the farm

Allyson: Hello William, how are you?

William: Hi Allyson, I'm fine, thank you. How were your holidays?

Allyson: Oh, they were really great! My family and I had a lot of fun.

William: Where did you go?

Allyson: Mum and Dad wanted to go the beach in Brighton or go visit my aunt in Manchester. But us kids didn't want to go there. Then I told them that I wanted to go to a farm close to London. I told them a lot about it, because my cousin was there last year. So we went to the farm. That was really great! There were so many animals: chickens, ducks, horses, ponies, sheep, goats, cows, and a bull. And there were lots of things to do, for example feed the animals, have a picnic, and ride on tractors. It was never boring. And my parents really liked it, too.

William: How did you get to the farm?

Allyson: We couldn't take the train because the tickets were too expensive. And the bus was late. So we took the car and started at 4 o'clock in the afternoon.

William: And what did you do on the farm?

Allyson: We arrived at the farm on Friday evening. It was late, so we only took a look at all the animals. Dad really liked the sheep and the goats. Mum's favourite animals are ducks. So we went to see them next. They have their own little pond. After that we saw the ponies and horses. I love horses! Josephine liked the pigs. They were so funny when they played in the dirt. Liam liked the bull best of all because it was so big.

William: And what about Saturday?

Allyson: On Saturday I rode one of the horses. It was not too big. So it was perfect for me. Her name was Bessy. Here is a picture of her.

William: What a nice horse! What did Liam do all the time?

Allyson: Liam saw a big tractor on a field. So he went to the farmer and rode on the tractor with him. And they worked in the field together. He was so excited! After that we had a family picnic. Dad took a lot of photos. While we were eating, we saw a boy who ran away from the bull very fast because it was angry. He didn't see the pond and fell in it. Look, here is a photo of the bull.

William: Oh! Poor boy! The bull looks really angry. And what did you do on Sunday?

Allyson: We didn't have so much time on Sunday because we wanted to go home before lunch. So we only went to the hen house and the pigs to feed them and to take some photos of them. At half past eleven we waved the farmer goodbye and went home.

William: That sounds really great! I think I want to go to that farm too!